OSPREY
PUBLISHING

Fortresses of the Peninsular War 1808–14

Ian Fletcher · Illustrated by Chris Taylor

Series editors Marcus Cowper and Nikolai Bogdanovic

First published in Great Britain in 2003 by Osprey Publishing, Elms Court,
Chapel Way, Botley, Oxford OX2 9LP, United Kingdom.
Email: info@ospreypublishing.com

ISBN 1 84176 577 5

Editorial by Ilios Publishing, Oxford, UK (www.iliospublishing.com)
Maps by The Map Studio, Romsey, UK
Index by Alison Worthington
Design: Ken Vail Graphic Design, Cambridge, UK
Originated by Grasmere Digital Imaging, Leeds, UK
Printed and bound by L-Rex Printing Company Ltd

03 04 05 06 07   10 9 8 7 6 5 4 3 2 1

A CIP catalogue record for this book is available from the British Library.

FOR A CATALOGUE OF ALL BOOKS PUBLISHED BY OSPREY MILITARY
AND AVIATION PLEASE CONTACT:

Osprey Direct UK, P.O. Box 140, Wellingborough,
Northants, NN8 2FA, UK
E-mail: info@ospreydirect.co.uk

Osprey Direct USA, c/o MBI Publishing, P.O. Box 1,
729 Prospect Ave, Osceola, WI 54020, USA
E-mail: info@ospreydirectusa.com

www.ospreypublishing.com

Contents

Introduction

Napoleon Bonaparte once said that while fortresses would not stop an army, they would nevertheless retard its movements: nowhere was this proven more clearly than in the Iberian Peninsula during the Peninsular War from 1808 to 1814. Although it is often stated (with some justification) that the war began in 1807, this study takes 1808 as its starting point, since it deals with the sieges that involved Wellington's Anglo–Portuguese army.

Space precludes any detailed discussion of the events that led to the outbreak of war in Portugal and Spain. In brief, the war came about as a result of French incursions into Spain following Junot's invasion of Portugal in November 1807. However, following the occupation of Portugal, French troops continued to linger in Spain too. When the French suddenly seized Pamplona and Barcelona, and occupied Madrid, all Spain rose in protest and revolts occurred in certain parts of the country, notably in Asturias and in Madrid itself, where the infamous rising, later called 'the Dos de Mayo', was ruthlessly suppressed by French troops. With Spain occupied and its king under arrest in France, the junta turned to its old enemy Britain for help: in August 1808 a small British army under Sir Arthur Wellesley, the future Duke of Wellington, arrived in Portugal at the start of a campaign that would see it drive the French first from Portugal and then Spain, pushing them over the Pyrenees and into France, and ending the war with the bloody battle of Toulouse in April 1814.

During the six years of war, Wellington's army fought several hard battles and numerous smaller actions, but it was the bloody sieges that troubled him more than anything else in Spain. Indeed, the performance of his army during the sieges was probably the most disappointing aspect of what was otherwise an extremely successful campaign. In fact, the failed siege of Burgos in September and October 1812 provided Wellington with his only defeat in six years of war against the French in the Peninsula.

Spain was, in Napoleon's words, a country where 'large armies starve and small armies get swallowed up'. It was also – and still is – a country blessed with more than its fair share of castles and fortified towns, and it was this, combined with the nature of the geography of Spain and Portugal, that would conspire to give four fortresses in particular more significance than they might otherwise have had. These fortresses were Ciudad Rodrigo, Badajoz, Burgos and San Sebastián, all of

Sir Arthur Wellesley, First Duke of Wellington, 1769–1852. No one was more aware of the deficiencies of his engineer services than Wellington himself. Never a man to waste the lives of his men, Wellington was nevertheless forced to throw his men into the fiery breaches on more than one occasion, suffering great losses.

which played a vital role in the Peninsular War largely as a result of their strategically important positions. The first two of these fortresses guarded the only two routes between Spain and Portugal that ran east–west. They were truly 'the keys to Spain'. The struggle for these two great fortresses, in particular Badajoz, would present Wellington with his greatest challenges and would provide his infantry with some of their stiffest tests of the war. Burgos and San Sebastián, on the other hand, had less strategic importance. However, they threatened Wellington's lines of communication, and although they posed a different kind of threat, they required the same remedy – a siege and storming.

The storming of a fortress inevitably ensured heavy casualties for the attackers, and there were no exceptions when Wellington's men were asked to carry out such tasks. However, it need not have been the case. Indeed, the custom of the day dictated that, in the event that practicable (that is to say, passable) breaches were made in the walls of a fortress, the garrison was required to surrender and march out with the honours of war. Unfortunately, Napoleon had decreed that none of his garrison commanders should surrender a fortress without sustaining at least one assault. The results of this policy will be dealt with later on. We will also examine not only the details of sieges and storming fortresses, but also the general role of the fortresses in Spain and see what impact they had on the thinking of the commanders and strategies of the armies involved. The relative inadequacy of both artillery and engineer arms of the British Army in the Peninsula will also be covered, a major contributory factor which caused Wellington to refer to these operations as 'sheer bludgeon work'.

The storming of Badajoz, after a painting by Caton Woodville. 'The storming of Badajoz affords as strong an instance of the bravery of British troops as has ever been displayed. But I earnestly hope I shall never again be the instrument of putting them to such a test as that to which they were put last night.' This was Wellington's own tribute to his magnificent men after the terrible assault on Badajoz. The great toil, the severe losses, the tremendous bravery of his men, and their savage explosion of anger afterwards, typified the siege operations in the Peninsula.

Chronology

The magnificent fortress town of Almeida in Portugal. The fortress sits just across the Portuguese border and, along with Ciudad Rodrigo, guards the northern corridor between that country and Spain. It was besieged in August 1810 by the French and fell following the great explosion when a shell ignited the powder magazine. A classic Vauban-type fortress, the fortifications are a fine example of 18th-century military science.

30 October: The French evacuate Portugal.

8 November: Napoleon enters Spain with 200,000 men.

4 December: Napoleon occupies Madrid.

10 December: Moore advances from Salamanca.

21 December: Paget's British cavalry is victorious at Sahagun. He follows this up with another victory, at Benavente, on 29 December.

1809

16 January: The Battle of Corunna. The British Army defeats Soult at Corunna, but Moore is mortally wounded. The victory allows the British to sail back to England.

22 April: Wellesley returns to Portugal and is once again in command.

12 May: Wellesley captures Oporto. Soult is thrown out of Portugal.

27–28 July: Wellesley achieves a costly victory at Talavera. He is rewarded with a peerage, and the name 'Wellington'.

20 October: Wellington issues his Memorandum for the construction of the Lines of Torres Vedras.

1810

10 July: Ciudad Rodrigo falls to the French under Marshal Masséna.

24 July: Robert Craufurd and his Light Division are severely tested by the French at the River Coa.

26 August: Almeida is devastated by a huge explosion as the magazine blows up. The town surrenders to the French shortly afterwards.

27 September: Wellington defeats Ney and Masséna at Busaco.

9 October: Wellington's troops begin to take up positions in the Lines of Torres Vedras.

14 October: Masséna discovers the Lines of Torres Vedras and halts.

17 November: Masséna withdraws to Santarem.

Standing across the border in Spain, opposite Almeida, is the fortress of Ciudad Rodrigo. Its Moorish walls were never really improved, save for the cutting of embrasures for artillery. Instead, the outer defences were modernised, including a deep ditch and a faussebraie, complete with angled bastions at regular intervals. The faussebraie can clearly be seen in this photo, effectively dividing the ditch into two.

1811	**5 March:** Masséna begins his retreat north towards the River Mondego.
	10 March: Soult takes Badajoz.
	11 March: Combat at Pombal, the first in a series of fights between Wellington and the retreating French.
	3–5 May: Battle of Fuentes de Oñoro, Masséna's last battle in Spain ends in defeat for him and the effective end of the third French invasion of Portugal.
	6 May: Beresford begins the first British siege of Badajoz.
	11 May: Brenier abandons Almeida to Wellington.
	16 May: Beresford defeats Soult at Albuera.
	19 May–17 June: Second British siege of Badajoz, which ends in bloody failure.
1812	**8 January:** Siege of Ciudad Rodrigo begins.
	19 January: Wellington takes Ciudad Rodrigo by storm.
	February–March: Wellington's army moves south to lay siege to Badajoz for a third time.
	16 March: Third siege of Badajoz begins.
	6 April: Badajoz is assaulted by Wellington's infantry: the fortress falls at midnight, and the town is sacked over the following two days.
	22 July: Wellington defeats Marmont at Salamanca.
	12 August: Wellington enters Madrid.
	19 September: Wellington begins the siege of Burgos.
	22 October: Wellington abandons the siege of Burgos.
	22 October–19 November: Allied retreat to Portugal.
	19 November: The Allied army arrives at Ciudad Rodrigo.
1813	**3 June:** The Allied army crosses the Duoro.
	13 June: French forces abandon Burgos.
	21 June: Wellington defeats Joseph at Vittoria. He is created Field Marshal.
	25 July: Soult makes a counter-attack in the Pyrenees. Battles take place at Maya and Roncesvalles.
	28–30 July: Wellington defeats Soult at Sorauren.
	31 August: Graham takes San Sebastián by storm.
	7 October: Wellington crosses the Bidassoa into France.
	25 October: Pamplona surrenders.
	10 November: Wellington defeats Soult at the Battle of the Nivelle.
	9–12 December: Wellington defeats Soult at the Battle of the Nive.
	13 December: Soult is repulsed by Hill at St Pierre.
1814	**27 February:** Wellington defeats Soult at Orthés.
	6 April: Napoleon abdicates.
	10 April: Wellington defeats Soult at Toulouse.
	14 April: The French sortie from Bayonne.
	17 April: Soult surrenders.
	27 April: Bayonne surrenders.
	30 April: The Treaty of Paris is signed.

The evolution of the fortress

By the time of the Napoleonic Wars the art of fortification and siege warfare had become a very complicated science indeed. Elaborate forts and siege works and almost ritualistic methods of siege warfare had dominated the 17th century, particularly during the Thirty Years War, and by the time of the Napoleonic Wars the science had been elevated to an art form. There were hundreds of manuals and guides for officers on the art of attack and defence, manuals that would stand many of them in good stead whilst on campaign. Indeed, one has only to study the list of subscribers to some of the manuals to discover just how popular they were and how highly regarded by officers who might one day be faced with defending a church, village or fort.

However, although the art of fortification might have seemed complicated at the time of the Napoleonic Wars, the basic principles that had stood the test of time for centuries still held good. Fortification was, as one writer defined it, 'the art of putting any place or post whatever in a favourable state of defence; it [fortification] implies also the method of attacking and defending the same.'

A detailed examination of each of the great Iberian fortresses will follow later in this book, but to begin with it will be as well to examine briefly their evolution, exploring how they developed from Moorish times until the Napoleonic Wars. Needless to say, the construction and final appearance of these fortresses were generally little different to those built elsewhere in Europe: probably the main distinction was that they had evolved from early Moorish beginnings. While many of the great northern European fortresses were built from scratch, so to speak, based upon the principles laid down by the French engineer Vauban, castles and fortresses in Spain had been in existence for centuries in strategically important positions, usually guarding the borders between kingdoms, or protecting river crossings and main roads. With each new development in technology there followed a natural modernisation of the fortresses. It is something that can be easily witnessed at places such as Ciudad Rodrigo and Badajoz where the old Moorish defences can be seen alongside the much later Vauban elements of defence. Both of these fortresses held strategically important positions, which necessitated their modernisation. There were others, however, such as Avila, which did not. Thus, the visitor to Avila today will see much the same fortress as had been standing for centuries before the war: it was never modernised as it was never deemed important enough to warrant the expenditure, and thus did not witness any great siege operation. Indeed, Napoleonic artillery would have had no trouble whatsoever in breaching the walls.

The crucial element of height was always uppermost in the minds of the engineers who constructed the fortress towns in Spain, and indeed Europe: without this any besieging force would have an easy time gaining access. Hence, we find so many Spanish castles built upon hills. Of course, such fortresses were designed to keep out enemies armed with little more than battering rams or, if they were lucky enough, catapults or other forms of medieval 'artillery'. At best, an attacking force might have been blessed with siege towers, which at least gave them a chance of getting over the walls, but more often than not they relied on throwing up ladders in the hope that they might be able to get over by escalade. This was much the way of things for centuries, particularly throughout the Moorish occupation of a large part of Spain, which was finally ended in the late-15th century. But the *Reconquista*, as the ejection of the Moors from Spain is called, coincided with the development

This example of a moated fortress is Peronne in France. This fortress was taken by the Foot Guards during the advance to Paris after the Battle of Waterloo. The walls benefit from having a moat, something which none of the fortresses in the Peninsula had.

of gunpowder and cannons as effective siege weapons, a factor which would bring about a dramatic change in the design of fortresses not only in Spain but throughout Europe.

Of course, when the great fortresses in Spain were built to guard the border corridors, nobody had yet considered the possibility that one day powerful artillery might come along and undermine the actual position of a fortress. By the time of the Peninsular War the implications of a poorly sited fortress became all too clear. For example, at Ciudad Rodrigo, the walls were dominated by a hill that stood some 16ft higher than the walls. The garrisons were constantly labouring at a disadvantage: one of the main maxims of fortification was that the parapet of a work should not be commanded by any height or point whatsoever which stood within cannon-shot of the walls. There was little that could be done about this, however, which placed an even greater burden upon those whose job it was to defend the place.

Height alone could no longer be relied on to thwart besieging armies. The assailants would now attack not only with ladders and battering rams, but with heavy artillery, capable of throwing down the walls and opening up huge breaches. A radical rethink was therefore instigated as to how towns and forts could be developed or modernised in order to combat this new threat. At this point we should consider one important factor that would have a bearing on the story of fortresses in Spain – their position. It is important to consider this, as the engineers who endeavoured to put into practice Vauban's designs and ideas were forced to work with fortresses that had already been built, and whose position had been previously decided upon in an age when height was the prime consideration in the construction of a town's walls. Needless to say, it was impossible for subsequent engineers to move the towns and so they had to do their best with what was already in existence. Hence the focus was on the modernisation of existing works rather than the construction of new ones, such as took place at Ciudad Rodrigo, where the walls retained the original Moorish structure when bringing them into the new scheme of things. There were exceptions, such as the walls of Badajoz which were totally rebuilt and modernised. The major development in fortresses in Spain came in the 18th century, with a great deal of modernisation carried out according to the principles of Vauban. Towns were already encompassed by walls, often antiquated and dilapidated, but it was the advent of powerful artillery that caused these walls themselves to be given protection.

The main feature of the Spanish (and all other) fortresses was their ramparts – in effect, the walls. The ramparts were formed of earth, often up to 40–50ft thick, packed solid and faced with stone. On top of the ramparts embrasures were cut for guns to be mounted in them. More often than not, sections of town walls were divided into lengths separated by bastions, which themselves were usually formed of four angled walls protruding from the walls themselves, the bastions being shaped so as to deflect artillery fire. Between the bastions themselves was the connecting wall, called the curtain. It was quite clear that although these walls and bastions were immensely strong they were still at

The flat, Moorish walls of Ciudad Rodrigo, as seen from within the inner ditch. Save for the introduction of embrasures for artillery these walls had remained the same for years. They provided no protection whatsoever against modern artillery. The walls were never modernised, angled or improved. Only the raising of the glacis and the building of the faussebraie gave the town any degree of protection during the Peninsular War.

the mercy of artillery firing straight at them and thus required protection themselves. It was deemed necessary, therefore, to build strong ravelins to protect the walls, and in particular the curtain, which was deemed to be the weak point. Ravelins were shaped very much like the bastions, with the angle pointing forward to deflect artillery. Both curtain walls and the bastions, tremendously thick and solid, with masonry securing thousands of tons of earth packed solidly within them, were now protected. However, even these immensely strong walls, bastions and ravelins were still considered to be at risk from heavy guns and explosive shells, and so all of these elements were protected in turn by a high glacis (the sloping ground directly in front of the fortress, separated from the walls by the ditch) that often shielded them and hid them completely from the view of enemy artillery. A good example of this is Fort San Cristobal, situated on the northern bank of the Guadiana River opposite Badajoz, which is completely hidden from view by the steep, sloping glacis and is not visible until one is actually standing at the very end of the glacis.

The ditches around the fortress walls usually caused besieging armies the most trouble. Sited at the end of the glacis, a ditch could be anything from 10–20ft deep, sometimes even deeper: storming columns would have to descend into this before assaulting the actual walls. Naturally, a garrison commander would see to it that the ditches were death traps, and ensure they remained completely clear of rubble or anything that might give cover to the attackers. The ditches were sometimes filled with water and at the very least had a smaller ditch, called a cunette, cut into the bottom of them. At Badajoz, for example, this was filled with water, whereas at smaller forts, such as Fort Conception, it was small and dry, and was designed simply with a view to causing as much trouble as possible to an attacking force. The cunette was not intended to stop an attacking force per se, but in the dark would certainly cause broken ankles or legs and other mishaps.

The walls of the 'castle' at Badajoz. In fact, there is no castle but a Moorish *alcazar* (or walled enclosure). These walls were taken by escalade by Picton's 3rd Division during the assault on 6 April 1812.

Another development brought about by the advent of effective artillery was the so-called 'outwork'. Some of the Spanish fortresses, such as Ciudad Rodrigo, Burgos, and Badajoz, were overlooked by higher ground which in medieval times may have presented little threat to the main fortress walls. However, with the arrival of effective artillery these hills suddenly assumed far greater significance and were immediately identified as weak points. It was deemed necessary, therefore, to build small forts or redoubts on such hills to prevent the enemy from siting their guns there. At Burgos, the heights of St Michael overlooked the castle, whilst at Ciudad Rodrigo the Upper Teson completely dominated the town. In both cases, forts were constructed to ensure the safety of the main work and to deny the positions to the enemy. The fortress city of Badajoz was not dominated directly, but it was overlooked from a height situated on the left bank of the Guadiana River: a strong fort, the San Cristobal, was constructed in order to prevent the enemy from taking advantage of this lofty position. The Fort San Cristobal was in turn dominated by a hill a few hundred yards to the north that had been left open. When Wellington arrived in June 1811, therefore, his engineers were quick to seize the position and site the Allied artillery there. When the siege was abandoned, the French quickly built a small fort on the heights to ensure the same process was not repeated if the Allies ever returned. At Ciudad Rodrigo, the threat posed by the heights of the Upper Teson was not lost on Wellington, who had used them to great effect during his successful siege of January 1812. Therefore, once the place was in his own hands he quickly had four forts built on top of the hill to prevent the French from using the position, not that the situation ever occurred.

A further characteristic of Vauban fortresses was the manner in which the fire from the bastions interlinked, creating a deadly crossfire. This was achieved largely through the elaborate symmetrical construction of each fortress, the sort of which may be seen all over northern Europe. However, there were those who considered these beautifully constructed forts too elaborate, for example, the French general Gaudi. He thought that in their quest for the perfect form, many officers had forgotten the true purpose of the fort. Forts were intended to be functional, not aesthetically beautiful, and did not need the incredible

Ciudad Rodrigo, drawn shortly after Wellington's men had stormed the town on 19 January 1812. The faussebraie can be seen, damaged in front of the Great Breach (right). The Great Breach was attacked by the 3rd Division whilst the Lesser Breach (to the left) was stormed by the Light Division.

The Moorish walls of the castle at Badajoz. Unlike the Moorish walls at Ciudad Rodrigo, these walls did at least have the added improvement of towers and these angled fronts, which afforded flanking fire. A low bank was built around the foot of the walls, which stand high on a hill and are not easily reached with artillery. Nevertheless, Wellington's gunners made a breach here in 1811. It was also at this point that Picton's 3rd Division scaled the walls on the night of 6 April 1812 during the great assault.

attention to detail that they were frequently afforded: so long as all angles of approach were covered, they did not need to be works of art. Gaudi wrote in 1804:

We have works of the same kind that assume many different figures, but they are all of them nearly of a like nature with those I have been describing above; and I am very sorry to say, of more show than of real utility; for although it is not to be doubted that the lines of all field-works should be broken, in order to procure a cross-fire, yet it must be owned that stars constructed methodically offer no real advantage from the regularity of their figure, and should be considered objects of mere speculation. It is certain that they are of much less utility and service than those works whose both sides and angles are unequal, but from which every surrounding object may be entirely discovered, and therefore defended in a direct line and by a cross-fire. Redoubts with such very important advantages will always be able to make a good defence.

He was quite right, of course, although much of his criticism referred to the construction of fieldworks and forts, rather than actual walled towns. It is certainly the case in Spain that there was not much over-elaboration at all. Indeed, when we come to examine each of the fortresses in turn, we will see how engineers incorporated many natural features into the overall defensive scheme of things at each site.

Fortress Spain

Some of the bloodiest episodes of the Peninsular War involved siege, storming and sacking. One of the most tragic was at Zaragoza, where thousands of innocent Spanish civilians died from sickness and hunger as a result of a prolonged siege by the French. On the other hand, some fortresses, such as Elvas in Portugal, were never besieged whilst Badajoz was the scene of three major sieges, by both French and British troops. There were several sieges in Spain and Portugal, from Tarifa in the south to San Sebastián in the north, but in this book we will focus on the 'big four', those of Ciudad Rodrigo, Badajoz, Burgos and San Sebastián in greatest detail.

The main fortresses in the Peninsula, and the five siege operations that took place there. Also shown are the key routes between France, Spain and Portugal that these fortresses protected.

Location

The geography of Spain and Portugal dictated that the two east–west corridors between the two countries would need to be protected by fortified towns, not only on the Spanish side of the border but on the Portuguese side also. The northern corridor was guarded by the twin fortresses of Ciudad Rodrigo in Spain and Almeida in Portugal. A lesser work, Fort Conception, situated less than a mile inside Spain, also covered the old road between the two countries. This fort, however, does not figure prominently in the annals of Peninsular sieges, and had a relatively short lifespan, of just 80 years, from 1730 until it was blown up by the British in 1810. The southern corridor between the two countries was similarly controlled by twin fortresses, Badajoz in Spain and Elvas in Portugal. In the north, the town of Burgos watched over the great road from Madrid to France. However, unlike the two great fortresses on the Portuguese border, Burgos was not a walled town. The object of Wellington's attention when he arrived there in September 1812 was the castle, situated high above the town. Further north lay the last great fortress in Spain, San Sebastián. Like Burgos, it commanded the road to France. Further inland was the fortress of Pamplona, which commanded the central route through the Pyrenees, where the road south from the great French military base of St Jean Pied de Port finally emerged from the mountains. On the east coast of Spain lay the fortresses of Barcelona, Gerona, Figueiras and Zaragoza, which commanded the eastern route out of France, through the Pyrenees and south into Spain.

A tour of the fortresses

Ciudad Rodrigo

The town of Ciudad Rodrigo witnessed a siege by the French in 1810 and by Wellington's army two years later. Situated on the right bank of the Agueda River, which lay to the west of the town and made any approach from this side impossible, it was relatively easy to attack on all three of the other sides. Its fortifications had been developed over the years, based upon early foundations constructed by the Moors. Prior to the advent of artillery, the strength of Ciudad Rodrigo lay in its position high on a hill, which made it difficult for enemy troops to attack the walls. However, once artillery came into its own Ciudad Rodrigo immediately found itself at the mercy of the dominating Upper Teson, a hill situated 600 yards to the north of the town and one which was 13ft higher than the walls. This was its real weakpoint: from here the walls were unprotected. Not even ravelins would have been able to protect them, given the steep-sided approach to the walls on the north side of the town.

When the French took Ciudad Rodrigo in 1810 they immediately set about building a small fort, called the Redoubt Renaud, on the forward edge of the Upper Teson, in order to prevent Wellington from using the hill. It was a good idea, but British troops stormed the redoubt on the first night of the siege in January 1812. After the capture of the town by Wellington, he immediately ordered no fewer than four forts to be constructed on the Upper Teson. If the French did ever return he was going to make certain that they used up valuable time in taking out these four forts. The forts had strong ditches and palisades to the rear: although they would not have been able to hold out for long, they would have bought the garrison valuable time and would have delayed the French attack. There was also a smaller hill much lower down between the Upper Teson and the town: it was called the Lower Teson, and was situated 180 yards from the walls. It did not dominate to the extent that the Upper Teson did, but it did allow enemy artillery to get extremely close with their guns. The soil on the two Tesons also marked them down as the obvious point of approach, as the ground on the other sides of the town was extremely hard and rocky, where digging would have proved difficult.

In addition to the threat posed by the Upper Teson, Ciudad Rodrigo was not blessed with particularly strong walls. The old Moorish walls there were never modernised in accordance with Vauban's principles, and at the time of the Peninsular War they still comprised poorly maintained masonry and were in an almost identical state to when they were first constructed centuries before. There were no bastions, flanks or angles, and not even any ravelins to protect the walls: they were completely at the mercy of enemy artillery. The only concession to modern warfare was the cutting of several embrasures on top of the ramparts in order for guns to be placed. Instead of modernising the walls, Spanish engineers evidently decided instead to bolster the town's defences by creating a faussebraie, that is to say a large, solid bank of earth sited in the ditch. This effectively created two ditches, the outer one being covered by a relatively effective glacis. This meant that the besieger's artillery would have to breach not only the walls themselves but the faussebraie as well. It also meant that attacking infantry would have to mount two obstacles instead of one. The faussebraie may well have been considered a rather effective obstacle to infantry but it was sited too far down the glacis to give the town's walls any real cover, and given the absence of any ravelins to protect the walls their poor positioning proved to be a critical error. Ironically, the faussebraie did have ravelins, albeit small ones on the south-east side of the town, although this side of the town was not chosen as the point of attack either by Masséna or by Wellington.

There was also a suburb outside the town which the Spaniards had tried to enclose within a poor earthwork; and four fortified convents, three within the suburb and one, the Santa Cruz, to the north-west of the town. This suburb would not present much of a threat to Ciudad Rodrigo as it was difficult to approach the town from that direction. Nevertheless, when Wellington arrived before the walls of the town in January 1812, Barrie, the French governor, saw

A plan of Ciudad Rodrigo, showing the siege lines of 1812. The map clearly shows how the town was protected from attack to the south by the River Agueda, and dominated to the north by the Upper Teson.

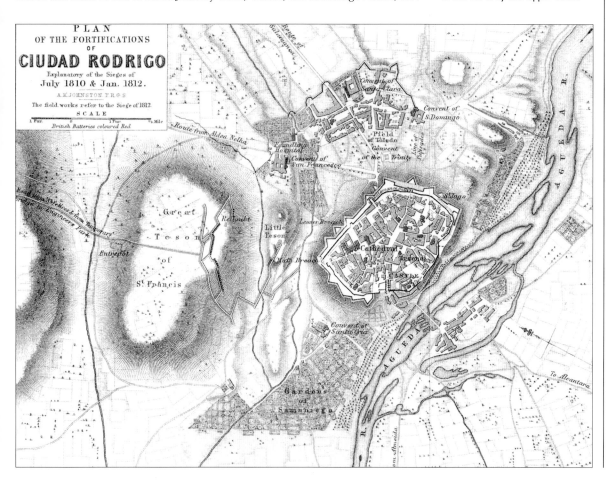

PLAN
OF THE FORTIFICATIONS
OF
CIUDAD RODRIGO
Explanatory of the Sieges of
July 1810 & Jan. 1812.
A.K.JOHNSTON F.R.G.S
The field works refer to the Siege of 1812.
SCALE
British Batteries coloured Red.

Ciudad Rodrigo, 1812

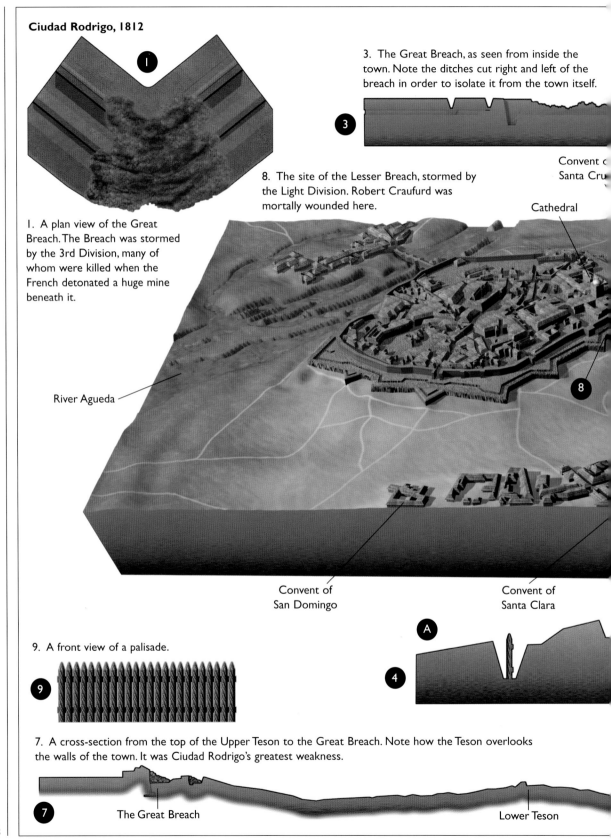

1. A plan view of the Great Breach. The Breach was stormed by the 3rd Division, many of whom were killed when the French detonated a huge mine beneath it.

3. The Great Breach, as seen from inside the town. Note the ditches cut right and left of the breach in order to isolate it from the town itself.

8. The site of the Lesser Breach, stormed by the Light Division. Robert Craufurd was mortally wounded here.

Convent of Santa Cru...

Cathedral

River Agueda

Convent of San Domingo

Convent of Santa Clara

9. A front view of a palisade.

7. A cross-section from the top of the Upper Teson to the Great Breach. Note how the Teson overlooks the walls of the town. It was Ciudad Rodrigo's greatest weakness.

The Great Breach

Lower Teson

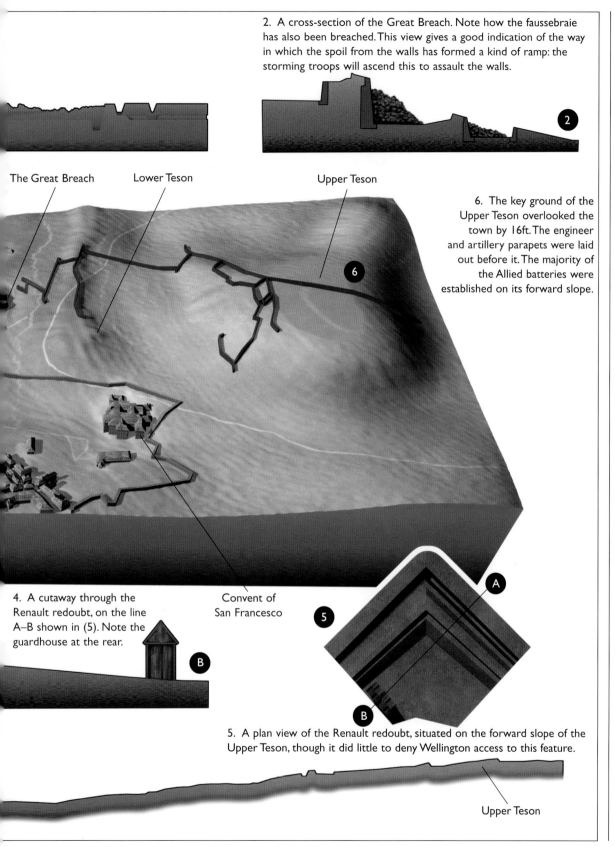

2. A cross-section of the Great Breach. Note how the faussebraie has also been breached. This view gives a good indication of the way in which the spoil from the walls has formed a kind of ramp: the storming troops will ascend this to assault the walls.

The Great Breach   Lower Teson   Upper Teson

6. The key ground of the Upper Teson overlooked the town by 16ft. The engineer and artillery parapets were laid out before it. The majority of the Allied batteries were established on its forward slope.

4. A cutaway through the Renault redoubt, on the line A–B shown in (5). Note the guardhouse at the rear.

Convent of San Francesco

5. A plan view of the Renault redoubt, situated on the forward slope of the Upper Teson, though it did little to deny Wellington access to this feature.

Upper Teson

A view of Badajoz, as seen from the south. The Roman bridge over the Guadiana can be seen at left, as can Fort San Cristobal, high on the hill, also to the left. This drawing was executed by Capt. C. Ellicombe, RE, during the third siege of Badajoz.

to it that the convents were turned into fortified posts that would require capturing before serious siege operations could begin.

In all, Ciudad Rodrigo was not a strong fortress. Its design and position may have been acceptable in the age of El Cid and the Moors, but its weaknesses were fatally exposed when the age of artillery dawned, particularly with the Upper Teson overlooking the walls at a range of just 600 yards. Its antiquated walls bore all the hallmarks of neglect by successive Spanish governors who were over reliant upon the ability of its garrison to withstand a siege, and on the only modern feature of the town's defences, the faussebraie. As we shall see later, neither the abilities of both Spanish and French garrisons, nor the faussebraie, were able to save the town from changing hands on two occasions.

Badajoz

Unlike the relatively weak Ciudad Rodrigo, Badajoz proved to be the hardest nut of them all for Wellington's men to crack. It was a fortress that would deny them in June 1811 and would almost do so again in April the following year, when they suffered severe casualties in storming the place. The city, situated on the banks of the wide River Guadiana, possessed extremely strong walls at the time of the Peninsular War. With the river protecting the northern side of the city it was not deemed necessary to build strong walls on this side: when the Moors built the walls back in the 12th century, they made them relatively low there, appreciating even then that it would be virtually impossible to attack the city from that direction. By the time of the Peninsular War, however, the walls had been not only been modernised but almost totally rebuilt, and outer defences constructed in order to withstand artillery. It was a fortress that Vauban himself would have been proud of.

The fortifications around the city consisted of eight massive bastions, linked together by immensely strong walls, with a ninth adjoining the old castle

Another view of Badajoz, again drawn by Capt. Ellicombe. This drawing was done from within Fort Picurina. The inundation, or false lake, can clearly be seen, being the light coloured area running across the middle distance in front of the town walls. The castle can be seen on the hill on the right of the drawing.

enclosure. The walls themselves varied from 20–46ft in height with embrasures cut into the top of the ramparts. Not only was the glacis extremely effective, but there were ravelins to protect each of the curtain walls. The French governor Phillipon, not content with the strength of the walls themselves, chose to utilise the Rivellas stream, which flowed along the eastern side of the city: a lunette (or fort), the San Roque, was situated here, and so Phillipon constructed a dam at this location which prevented the Rivellas from flowing into the Guadiana. By doing so a lake, or inundation, was created, which would cause Wellington great problems when he attacked in March and April 1812. Instead of being able to attack the breaches head-on, his attacking columns had to move across the face of them, exposing their left to the fire of the defenders. Phillipon also let water into the ditch in front of the breach in the Trinidad bastion, to form a kind of moat. This too would cause many casualties amongst Wellington's attacking troops.

Situated upon the highest point of the city was the castle, the former Moorish *alcazar*. This was really more of an enclosure than a castle, being encircled by a wall. When the French were besieged in 1812, Phillipon chose to make the castle his place of last refuge and piled his stores into it. Ironically, it would be the first post to fall. Along this northern side of the city, the Moorish walls had been retained and incorporated into the city's defences, it being considered unlikely that the enemy would attack in these sectors. Indeed, the hill was around 120ft high, which mostly protected the castle from artillery fire, although Wellington's gunners did nevertheless make a breach in the castle walls from distances of 650 and 800 yards. When the city was assaulted in April 1812, Wellington's men

The great fortress of Badajoz, showing the lines of the siege of 1812. The large outworks of forts Pardaleras and Picurina can clearly be seen, built on the high ground to the south and south-east.

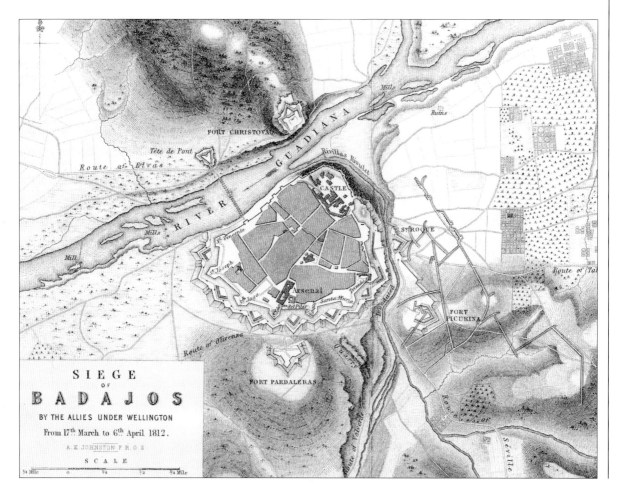

SIEGE
OF
BADAJOS
BY THE ALLIES UNDER WELLINGTON
From 17th March to 6th April 1812.
A.K.JOHNSTON F.R.G.S
SCALE

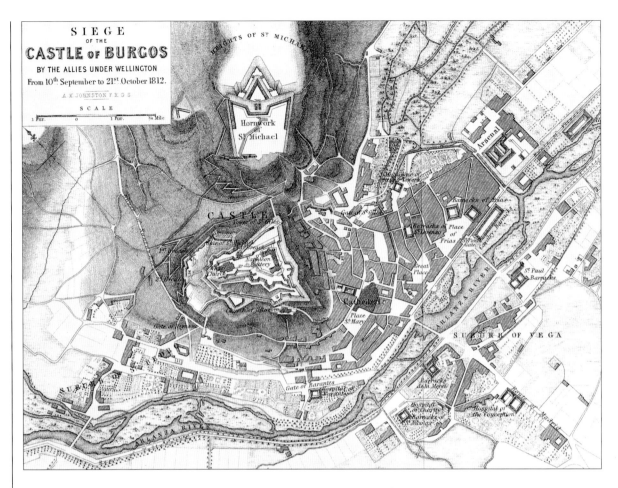

SIEGE
OF THE
CASTLE of BURGOS
BY THE ALLIES UNDER WELLINGTON
From 10th September to 21st October 1812.

A.K.JOHNSTON F.R.G.S.

SCALE

A plan of Burgos, showing Wellington's siege lines of September and October 1812. As can be seen, the town itself is open and without walls. Wellington's operations were directed against the castle and the hornwork to the north. It proved to be too much for Wellington, however, and was his one great failure of the Peninsular War.

attacked the castle by means of escalade, this being considered the only possible way of gaining entry at this point. The great historian of the sieges, Col. John Jones, thought that Phillipon had neglected the defences here. There had been plans for improvements but nothing was done. For example, only two guns had been mounted on the ramparts. It is possible that Phillipon considered the position so strong that the notion of it being taken by the enemy was inconceivable.

Like Ciudad Rodrigo, Badajoz was prone to attack from two elevated positions. These were two fairly low hills that lay to the south and south-east: whilst not overlooking the city in the same way that the Upper Teson overlooked Ciudad Rodrigo, it was nevertheless considered necessary to build forts upon them. Thus the French constructed Fort Picurina, 400 yards from the walls, and Fort Pardaleras, 200 yards away. It was no mean achievement taking the first of these two forts, whilst the second was not taken until the town actually fell by assault on 6 April 1812. However, it was never Wellington's intention to place his guns on the hill occupied by Fort Pardaleras. Fort Picurina, on the other hand, held the key to Badajoz, being sited at the perfect location from where the breaching batteries would open fire.

Across the River Guadiana there stood another height upon which the Spaniards had constructed Fort San Cristobal. Located just 500 yards from the city itself, the fort was an important part of the city's defences, so important in fact that its capture would severely compromise the city itself. When Wellington attacked Badajoz in June 1811 his main objective was to capture the fort, which he hoped would force Phillipon and his garrison to surrender. Fort San Cristobal was extremely strong: it could only be approached from the north, as the ground sloped steeply down to the river on its south side, a ravine protected its eastern approach, and any approach from the west would be compromised not only by the garrison in the *Tête-de-Pont*, the fort situated at the northern end of the bridge across the Guadiana but also by the fact that the ground fell away. The ditch itself is 14ft deep and was a death trap for any assailants, as was proved when Wellington's men attacked in June 1811. The ground was also extremely hard and rocky, making it virtually impossible to dig trenches. The only possible location for enemy breaching batteries was on the hill to the north, and no sooner had Wellington abandoned the siege than the French came out and constructed a fort upon it, called the Lunette Werle, after the French general killed at Albuera in May 1811. Like forts Picurina and Pardaleras, the fort would prevent Wellington from using the hill against Fort San Cristobal.

With massive walls, powerful defences, and (equally importantly) an aggressive commander supported by an able staff and tenacious garrison, Badajoz was the strongest of the four fortresses attacked by Wellington. Although there were no obvious weak points, it is significant that the one place where the defences had been identified by Jones as having been neglected proved Phillipon's undoing, although even he must have been as shocked as anyone when Picton's 3rd Division managed to scale the walls and get over. Perhaps we should forgive him this oversight; after all, there is always the unexpected and no matter how good the arrangements made by a garrison commander, if the besiegers possess such troops as will overcome anything thrown against them, there is little he can do.

Burgos

The town of Burgos, situated on the main road from Madrid to France via San Sebastián, commanded the crossing points of the River Arlanzón: it was different to Ciudad Rodrigo and Badajoz in that it was not a walled fortress. Instead, it was an open town with the castle stronghold placed high upon a hill overlooking the town. It had become a French depot during the Peninsular War but owing to the fact that the war never really came anywhere near, the French neglected to improve its ageing defences. And yet it was the one place that withstood Wellington's attacks.

The massive bank of the third line of defences at Burgos, seen from the north. Behind the line the walls of the castle itself can just be seen.

The castle itself was not a particularly strong site, with relatively weak walls, no bastions or ravelins to protect them, and no real glacis. However, it was encircled by three defined 'lines' (earthworks). The third or upper line surrounded the castle itself along with a church, La Blanca. The line was in effect a retrenchment, but a strong and deep one, some 30ft wide. The castle keep itself had been incorporated into the third line as an interior retrenchment mounting a well protected battery named after Napoleon. The second line encompassed this third line completely. Once again it was a retrenchment with strong palisades in the ditch. The lower or outer line extended along the northern and north-west front of the castle, being connected to the second line on its east and west fronts. It was sited much lower down than the other lines with palisades protecting the flanks and re-entrants. These three lines, whilst not having any great strength, had the benefit of height and the slopes before the castle made entrenching very difficult. The down side of this was that the slopes were so steep in places that it was difficult for the defenders to depress their guns adequately to fire on their assailants.

Some 300 yards to the east of the castle, and separated from it by a deep ravine, was the hill of St Michael. It was on the same level as the castle and thus posed a great threat to it. For this reason, a large, three-sided hornwork was built upon it, with an open back enclosed with palisades. The sides of the hornwork were 25ft high and had a ditch some 10ft deep. It was entirely covered by the fire of the guns in the Napoleon battery.

One of the drawbacks of the castle's isolated position was the shortage of water. No fortification can hold out without it, and as it had to be drawn from the town it soon became in short supply when Wellington surrounded the place in 1812. Otherwise, the place was fairly well provisioned.

Burgos's defences were nowhere near as strong as those of either Ciudad Rodrigo or Badajoz and it was not regarded as a particularly daunting prospect by Wellington's men. The position of the castle, situated as it was upon a hill, did not lend itself to any of the principles of defence laid down by Vauban. Its strength lay in its elevated position, and in the event, the defences proved more than adequate to keep Wellington at bay in 1812, aided by bad weather and Wellington's underestimation of the place's strength. As we shall see, he undertook the siege operation with woefully inadequate artillery. It was to prove his only real failure in the Peninsula.

The strong walls of the eastern side of the castle of Burgos are pictured here. No attacks were made against this section of the walls.

San Sebastián

San Sebastián is situated on an isthmus jutting into the Bay of Biscay: Monte Urgullo, which occupies the northern end of the isthmus, looks down on to the town below. On the very top of Monte Urgullo stands a castle that played no prominent role in the 1813 siege other than to afford refuge to the retreating French garrison when the town fell to the Allies. San Sebastián was a walled town in 1813. Its main defences lay in front of the town, that is to the south, where a large hornwork covered the whole south face of the walls. Behind the hornwork, the walls were protected at either end by a bastion and by a cavalier, that is to say, a smaller raised bastion, in the centre. The curtain wall was covered by a glacis, with a covered way and a ditch. The walls to the east and west of the town were simply curtain walls, with no bastions, glacis or counterscarps, due to the fact that the River Urumea was located to the east whilst the sea lapped up against the western wall.

San Sebastián would therefore appear to have been impregnable to attack from all but one side, the south. The truth was, however, that the French placed far too much trust in the natural defence of both river and sea: their complacency would prove fatal. It was certainly true to say that the River Urumea was not passable for most of the day, but at low tide the mouth of the river was easily fordable. Furthermore, the eastern wall was exposed to fire from two directions: the Chofre sand hills some 500 yards away to the east, and Monte Olla 1,000 yards away to the north-east. Given that the eastern wall had no protection in the form of ravelins or bastions, it was most certainly a weak point.

A plan of San Sebastián and the siege operations of June to September 1813.

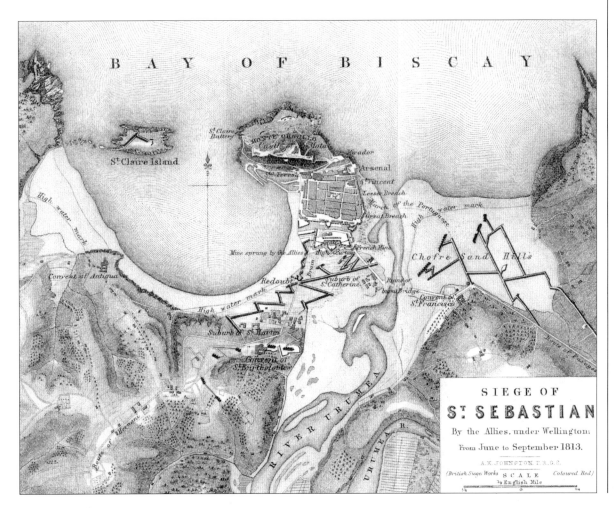

SIEGE OF

St SEBASTIAN

By the Allies, under Wellington;

From June to September 1813.

A.K. JOHNSTON, F.R.G.S.

(British Siege Works   S C A L E   Coloured Red.)

⅓ English Mile

San Sebastián, as drawn by Wilkinson in 1835. The town's fortifications had not changed much in the 20 years since Wellington's men stormed the place on 31 August 1813. The castle to which Governor Rey and the survivors of his garrison retreated can clearly be seen on top of Monte Urgullo, in the background on the right.

The narrow isthmus presented an attacking force with the problem of having to attack on a narrow frontage. Indeed, the spit of land in front of the hornwork was not more than 500 yards across, whilst any attacking troops would have to issue from a piece of ground not more than 300 yards in breadth. It was a very narrow front indeed. However, the river mouth at low tide partly solved this problem, although even here attacking troops storming the place from the east would be exposed to the fire of the defenders from the moment they left their trenches until they finally reached the walls, a distance of over 1,000 yards.

San Sebastián was well provisioned, with French ships gaining access to the harbour during the early days of the siege until the Royal Navy finally cut it off: even then, smaller boats managed to get through on occasion. There was never really any chance of an attacking force starving the garrison into surrender. With France being so close, the Allies were also exposed to the risk of relief forces arriving from behind in order to get through to the garrison: Marshal Soult tried exactly this in August 1813, although without success.

San Sebastián was therefore a strong fortress, which made use of its natural barriers as well as its man-made fortifications, all of which had been modernised during the 18th century. Ironically, these strong points were compromised during certain times of the day when the tide was out. Otherwise, the fortress could be considered one of the strongest in Spain. Its close proximity to France gave it an added strategic importance, and it was used as a major French base for most of the war. Sadly, it was, along with Badajoz, sacked in the most savage manner when it fell to Wellington's men in 1813 during an attack made all the worse by a fire which virtually destroyed the entire town.

The principles of defence

There was really only one objective for the commander of a fortress's garrison. Quite simply, he had to keep the enemy out by using any means at his disposal. It was, therefore, essential that the defences of his fortress were in as effective a state as was possible, otherwise he would begin the defence of his position under an immediate disadvantage. Sieges were frequently problems of time; that is to say, the besiegers would have only a certain amount of time to successfully capture a fortress before relieving troops arrived on the scene to put an end to the business. Each day, each hour even, that was gained by the defenders would allow the relief force time to approach closer and upset the plans of the besiegers. It was absolutely imperative, therefore, that the fortress's defences made the besiegers work hard for their prize. If the walls were in a dilapidated state it would not take long for enemy artillery to breach them. This was the case at the Portuguese fortress of Campo Mayor, for example, which the French took extremely quickly and easily in March 1811.

Of course, if there was no chance of a relief force interfering with siege operations, an attacking commander would have the relative luxury of taking his time and, if possible, starving the garrison into surrender. It was thus necessary for a garrison commander to accumulate a large store of supplies whenever a siege seemed likely. Such a store was usually accumulated in a safe building, not exposed to fire, such as a church, cathedral or castle, and it was not to be touched until the besiegers had entirely blockaded the town. 'Man cannot live by bread alone,' however, and a good, uncontaminated water supply was vital. Such wells were usually to be found in towns anyway.

The great angled form at the northern end of Fort San Cristobal, Badajoz. It was against this flank of the fort that Wellington vainly directed his efforts in June 1811.

No matter how good a condition the walls of a fortress were in, it was inevitable that sooner or later they would be breached and would become 'practicable', meaning it would be possible for storming troops to pass through into the town beyond. The garrison commander was therefore faced with two choices. He could either hold out for relieving troops (hopefully) to arrive, or he could make the besiegers pay for their prize with the blood of their troops. Given the inevitability of a storming, any commander who opted for the first course of action – or inaction – was playing an extremely dangerous game. To simply wait for an assault and hope to thwart the enemy's attack was sheer folly: the correct way was to be an aggressive garrison commander, launching sorties, encouraging the garrison, displaying vigour and seeing that the walls were repaired. By doing so, he could retard the besiegers' operations and could, with any luck, hope for relief. Such was the behaviour of the governor of Badajoz, Armand Phillipon, in June 1811.

Phillipon demonstrated all of the attributes of an aggressive commander and his attempts to thwart Wellington proved successful. The gallant defence of Fort San Cristobal led to Wellington abandoning the siege, one that had become a 'time problem' for him. When relief troops approached in strength, the Allies were forced to abandon the siege. This was largely thanks to the garrison and its commander who bought time for themselves through their sheer aggression. The same manner was adopted again in March and April 1812 when Wellington returned once more to lay siege to Badajoz. On this occasion not even Phillipon could keep Wellington's baying wolves from the door, but even then it was an extremely close call. A French relief force was only a matter of days away when Wellington's men stormed the town, at great cost to themselves.

At Ciudad Rodrigo in January 1812, the garrison commander, Barrie, showed himself to be the complete opposite, and apart from a single sortie relied upon the ability of his men to withstand the assault. He failed to buy any time for himself and thus Wellington was able to capture the town after just 11 days, without any interference from French forces elsewhere.

Another view of the ditch of Fort San Cristobal, Badajoz. This photo was taken from the covered way, beyond which stands a very effective glacis that almost completely covers the walls of the fort from artillery fire.

We may well take Phillipon at Badajoz, and indeed Governor Dubreton at Burgos, as examples of how to conduct a vigorous defence of a fortress. At Badajoz, Wellington's engineers identified the south-east side of the city as its weak point: this was not lost on the French, however, who had built Fort Picurina where Wellington's artillery would have wanted to site their guns. It was not until 25 March that the fort was stormed after a short but violent attack. Wellington was then able to place his guns inside the fort and open fire on the walls of the town – but this had cost him six valuable days. Dubreton also launched several successful sorties at Burgos and inflicted heavy casualties upon the besiegers. In fact, such was the aggressive conduct of Dubreton's defence that Wellington, pressed for time, was forced to abandon the siege: thus began the retreat from Burgos, a withdrawal which did not end until Wellington, who had hitherto enjoyed an otherwise tremendously successful year, had retired to Portugal.

Aggression alone would not save a garrison, though. It also required strong defences. The sort of defences conducted at Burgos and Badajoz began outside the walls of their respective strongholds, with sorties and with the fights for the outworks. But the real work was to be done at the walls themselves and in the area immediately in front of them. First, all scrub, trees and undergrowth would be cut down so as not to afford enemy troops any cover. Any suburbs would have to be destroyed also. After all, it was no use a garrison maintaining strong walls if they then allowed the enemy to get close with their artillery via the suburbs.

If he were lucky, a garrison commander would be afforded valuable help by the natural features of the ground upon which his fortress was situated. He would take advantage of streams and rivers to create dams and flood certain areas, as we have already noted. After drawing upon these natural barriers, the governor would then ensure that the fortress's man-made defences were in a state of good repair. It was vital that the condition of the glacis was maintained.

A view of Ciudad Rodrigo, as seen from the northernmost surviving fort on the Upper Teson. In the middle distance can be seen the other remaining fort. Despite being small, they would absorb both the attackers' time and energy and might make the difference between a capitulation and a relief. There were originally four forts, all of which were built by Wellington's men. This photo also shows quite clearly how the Upper Teson completely dominated the walls of the town.

29

Badajoz, 1812

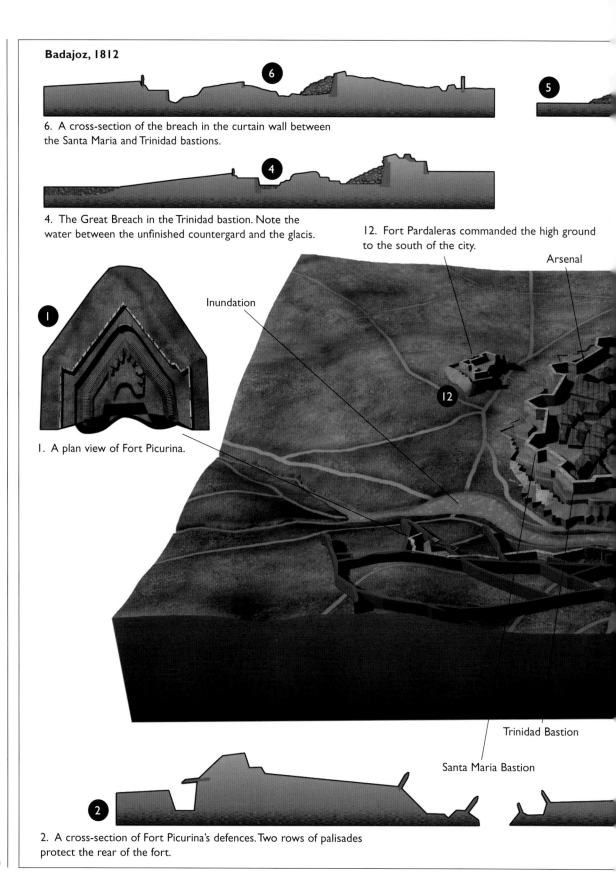

6. A cross-section of the breach in the curtain wall between the Santa Maria and Trinidad bastions.

4. The Great Breach in the Trinidad bastion. Note the water between the unfinished countergard and the glacis.

12. Fort Pardaleras commanded the high ground to the south of the city.

Arsenal

Inundation

1. A plan view of Fort Picurina.

Trinidad Bastion

Santa Maria Bastion

2. A cross-section of Fort Picurina's defences. Two rows of palisades protect the rear of the fort.

11. *Chevaux de frise* were placed across the breaches, making a formidable barrier.

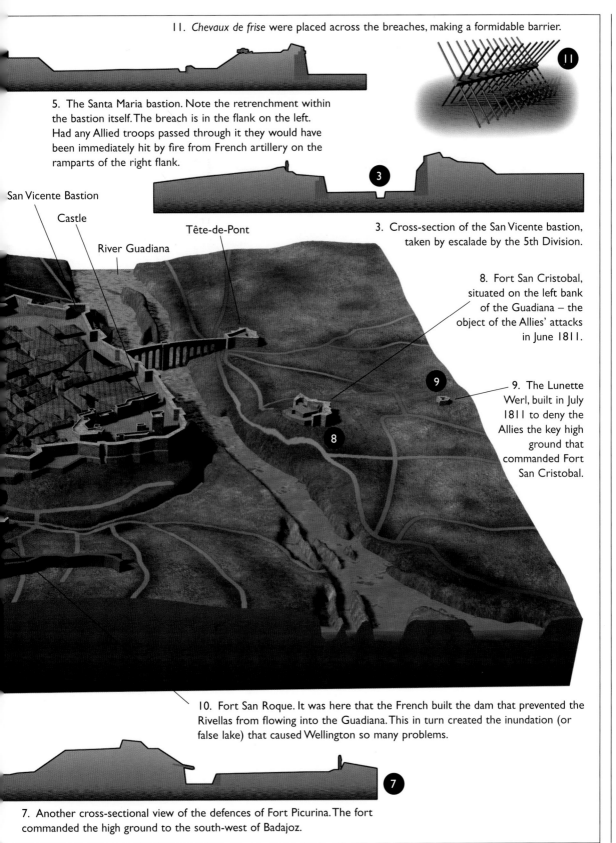

5. The Santa Maria bastion. Note the retrenchment within the bastion itself. The breach is in the flank on the left. Had any Allied troops passed through it they would have been immediately hit by fire from French artillery on the ramparts of the right flank.

San Vicente Bastion

Castle

River Guadiana

Tête-de-Pont

3. Cross-section of the San Vicente bastion, taken by escalade by the 5th Division.

8. Fort San Cristobal, situated on the left bank of the Guadiana – the object of the Allies' attacks in June 1811.

9. The Lunette Werl, built in July 1811 to deny the Allies the key high ground that commanded Fort San Cristobal.

10. Fort San Roque. It was here that the French built the dam that prevented the Rivellas from flowing into the Guadiana. This in turn created the inundation (or false lake) that caused Wellington so many problems.

7. Another cross-sectional view of the defences of Fort Picurina. The fort commanded the high ground to the south-west of Badajoz.

One of the surviving forts built by Wellington on the Upper Teson, overlooking Ciudad Rodrigo.

At Badajoz, Phillipon raised its height, so as to make it extremely difficult for Wellington's artillery to see the foot of the walls, its intended target: this was one of the main functions of the glacis. However, it was important that the glacis was not so steep as to prevent the defenders from seeing the attacking troops or to allow the same attackers a degree of cover. Often, a covered way was constructed along the top of the glacis to enable defenders to fire upon the attacking troops as they approached, although the defenders at all of the great fortresses in Spain remained inside during the respective assualts.

At the end of the glacis was the counterscarp, the technical word for the outer edge of the ditch nearer the glacis. But it was the condition of the ditch itself that was the main concern for both besieged and besieger. The ditch could be anything up to 30–40ft deep and twice as wide, often more. It was important that it be kept clear of rubble, for as far as the defenders were concerned it needed to be as deep as possible to further complicate the assault on the walls themselves. This was the killing ground, the defenders would have to destroy their assailants here. Often, the ditches would be mined, the fuses being lit just prior to an assault going in. The consequences for the storming columns were usually fatal. Indeed, it was not for nothing that the first troops sent in to assault the breaches were known as 'the forlorn hope'. As well as the use of mines, palisades were often employed in the ditches. These huge stakes were driven into the ground at the bottom and would frequently cause the attacking troops a great deal of trouble in breaking them down before they could pass on and attack the breaches. Ditches were often filled with water, particularly if a river or stream were close at hand. At Badajoz, the waters of the Rivellas stream were let into the ditch, and the flooded excavation caused Wellington's men scores of casualties, with many drowning as they leapt into the ditch in the dark.

On the other side of the ditch were the ramparts themselves, huge walls often 50–60ft high that had to be maintained and repaired, either with masonry or

with wood. Cut into the top of the ramparts were embrasures to allow guns to be emplaced. During a storming, defenders would crowd into these embrasures, firing into the night at their assailants gathered below. The ramparts were usually sloped, not only to deflect shot but also to allow defenders to roll shells, grenades and other combustibles over the edge and down into the ditch below. This proved extremely effective during the abortive attack on Fort San Cristobal at Badajoz in June 1811, when the small garrison inside the fort simply tossed every conceivable explosive device over the ramparts and into the ditch beneath them. It was a simple but very effective method of slaughter, which was achieved with no great danger to themselves.

No matter how confident a garrison commander was, he could never rule out the possibility of attacking troops passing through a breach in the walls,

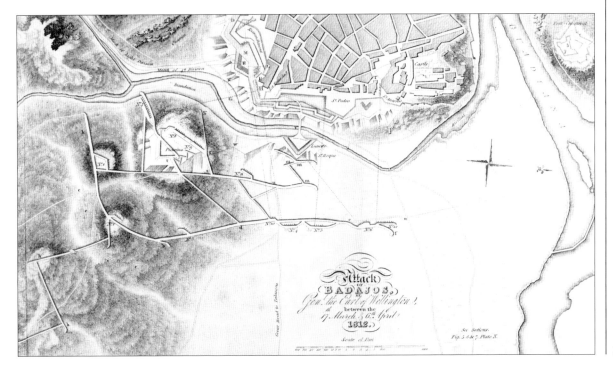

This painting by Caton Woodville, depicting Wellington at the breaches after the storming of Badajoz, shows the sort of savage means employed by the French in blocking the breaches. *Chevaux-de-frises*, formed of sword blades driven into timber beams, proved impassable to Wellington's stormers and prevented them from gaining the town, despite making as many as 40 separate attacks.

and any diligent commander would see to it that the houses immediately behind a breach were pulled down. A retrenchment would then be made across the rear of the breach, so that in the event of the storming troops passing through they would find themselves staring straight at many guns facing them from within the walls themselves. At Badajoz, for example, the Santa Maria bastion was retrenched with guns sited deep inside it, facing the rear of the breach from within.

A commander would also see to it that the breach was isolated from the town by digging a trench around it. At San Sebastián, for example, the storming parties finally won through the breach, only to find a 30ft excavated drop into the town. The same thing happened at Ciudad Rodrigo, where Barrie dug two deep trenches on either side of the rear of the breach, thus isolating it from the ramparts themselves.

But no matter how strong the walls and defences of a fortress were, it still needed a resolute and tenacious garrison behind them to keep out the enemy. The combination of both proved successful at Burgos and at Badajoz in 1811. The failure in 1812 was mainly due to the astonishing and awesome power of the storming troops and is no reflection on the prowess of the garrison and its commander.

The besieger and the besieged

During the two centuries prior to the Peninsular War, it had been the custom for the garrisons of fortresses whose walls had been breached to surrender after being instructed to do so by the besieging force. The garrison would then be allowed to march out with honour, having clearly done their duty. Naturally there were exceptions to this: indeed, the Thirty Years War was marked by protracted sieges with subsequent storming here and there. By the advent of the Napoleonic era, garrisons were not expected to fight to the death, but to cause as much trouble for the besieger as possible before giving in. However, as previously noted, one of Napoleon's decrees made it quite clear that none of his garrison commanders should surrender any town or fortress without having first sustained at least one assault by the enemy. This put his commanders most definitely on the spot, leaving each of them to face the very real possibility that, should the enemy launch a successful assault on walls that were deemed practicable by them, they could expect to be shown little mercy. Indeed, any successful storming troops were well within their rights to put the garrison to the sword.

Naturally, Napoleon's decree put immense pressure on garrisons – the true intent in any case – who were suddenly placed in the unenviable position of having a potential life or death situation thrust upon them. In Armand Phillipon, governor of Badajoz, we have an example of a man who rose to the challenge and who came extremely close to thwarting Wellington's objective in 1812, having already denied him the previous year. But one is given to consider how hard he would have fought if the governor of Ciudad Rodrigo, Barrie, had been put to the sword along with his garrison for fighting on despite Wellington having created practicable breaches in the walls of the town. The point is that by fighting on, Barrie technically waived all rights to mercy and risked having not only his career

This superb painting by Thomas St Clair shows the siege operations in progress at Badajoz. In the middle distance hundreds of British soldiers can be seen hacking away at the ground, digging the parallels, whilst others begin a new length at right. Parties of riflemen can be seen (left centre) marching out to occupy the rifle pits from where they fired upon the defenders in the gun embrasures on the walls.

but his life terminated by some extremely angry and agitated British soldiers who would have come through a severe test to win the town. Furthermore, it was a test they would have considered pointless given the condition of the walls, which they would have thought indefensible. Many of Wellington's men may appear to have been rather brutish and lacking in intelligence at times, but they were acutely aware of their rights following a successful storming, rights that allowed them to plunder a town and, more significantly as far as the garrison was concerned, slaughter the defeated defenders.

When Wellington's men assaulted the walls of Ciudad Rodrigo on the night of 19 January 1812, it was the first occasion they had taken a fortress by storm in the Peninsular War. Furthermore, as the great historian of the British Army Sir John Fortescue pointed out, it was the first time since Drogheda in 1649 that a British Army had stormed a regularly fortified European fortress. It is true that they had taken Monte Video by storm in February 1807, although the defences there were in a poor state of repair. Wellington himself had seen his men storm fortresses when, as Sir Arthur Wellesley, he had fought in India. But during the Napoleonic Wars British troops had yet to savour such success until the events at Ciudad Rodrigo – and nobody (Wellington included) had given much thought to what might happen afterwards. Officers were caught largely by surprise and were unable to stop their men dispersing inside the town in order to enjoy themselves. In the event, the men were also – fortunately – taken aback by this sudden break from rigid army discipline, and as a consequence the disorder was not particularly violent, nor was it prolonged. Within a few hours of Wellington's men gaining the town they were being rounded up and marched out again, along with the French garrison for whom the war was now over.

The significance of the garrison being allowed to march away as prisoners rather than ending the siege as lifeless corpses was not lost on the defenders of

A breach in one of the bastions of Fort Conception, near Almeida. The fallen debris forms a sort of ramp, up which the stormers would attack. The defenders would try to remove as much of this as possible in order to deny them the facility. They would also block the breach with all manner of obstacles.

Badajoz. They knew that when the time came for them to defend their own walls they could do so in the knowledge that even if they were unsuccessful they could kill as many of Wellington's men as possible without fear of retribution. Of course, they were not sure whether they would be put to the sword if they chose to fight on, but the fact that the garrison of Ciudad Rodrigo had been spared was a good indication that theirs was a calculated risk and not a suicidal course of action. The fact that Barrie's troops had been spared was not lost on Wellington either, for when the war was over he was left to reflect ruefully on what might have happened had his men slaughtered the entire garrison rather than just a contingent of Italians, who were the only defenders to have been shown no mercy. Wellington said if he had put the garrison of Ciudad Rodrigo to the sword he would have saved himself the flower of his army at Badajoz. He went on, chillingly; 'I say this to show that the slaughtering of a garrison is not a useless effusion of blood.'

The great irony was that, having taken Badajoz, the victorious British troops did nothing to exact their revenge against the defenders. There is little doubt that some French troops were killed afterwards but on the whole it was the population that suffered, as they were suspected of being pro-French. Badajoz was sacked mercilessly from top to bottom, with all manner of outrages being committed against the town and its population. Indeed, it remains one of the most shameful episodes in the history of the British Army.

The incentive for the French garrisons in Spain to fight on and resist, rather than meekly enter captivity, was very great indeed. Despite the fact that Wellington's men had refused to slaughter the garrison at Ciudad Rodrigo there was no guarantee that this fate would not befall the other garrisons at Badajoz, San Sebastián and Burgos. Even if they were spared following an unsuccessful

The spoil from the breached walls can clearly be seen in this painting by Atkinson, providing a convenient ramp for the Light Division during the storming of Badajoz, 6 April 1812.

The site of the Great Breach at Ciudad Rodrigo, with the actual breach at the right-hand edge of this photo. The flat walls illustrate perfectly just how easy it was to shoot down the entire length of the ditch. However, the walls afforded little protection against artillery fire. There are no ravelins or bastions, only a faussebraie to protect the walls.

defence, there was still the prospect of a long period of confinement aboard one of the dreaded prison ships, or hulks, moored off Cadiz or on the Medway in England, or in a damp, uncomfortable prison somewhere in England. The incentives were certainly something that Phillipon in particular played upon at Badajoz, issuing constant reminders of the terrible conditions aboard the prison ships.

Daily life inside the fortresses

It was important that the garrisons remained vigilant, not only to watch for any offensive moves by the enemy, but also to observe the progress of their works. Great use was made of church towers inside the towns as observation posts. This paid dividends at both Ciudad Rodrigo and Badajoz where the lookouts were able to make very pertinent observations on just how Wellington's men conducted their operations. For example, it was noted that, during the changeover between shifts by the troops working the trenches, the trenches remained unguarded. Sorties were then launched, the French troops filling in as much of the besiegers' trenches as possible and doing as much damage as they could before returning quickly to the safety of their walls. At Burgos, constant sorties by Dubreton's men caused Wellington's troops no end of problems and largely contributed towards the ultimate failure of the siege.

It was also important that each garrison remained active in repairing and improving the defences. If enemy artillery fire could not be prevented, a good garrison commander would at least see to it that its effects were limited by carrying out repair work as often as possible. Of course, this was ultimately akin to trying to empty a lake with a teaspoon – a thankless task. One beneficial thing they could do was to clear away as much of the rubble as possible at the foot of each breach. By doing this they deprived the storming troops of the sort of 'ramp' that was needed to facilitate their ascent through the breaches and into the town. Much of this work was done after dark, when defenders could work in relative safety.

Artillery fire was not employed by the besieging force after nightfall, it being impossible to see the target. But this did not mean that siege work stopped altogether. Digging went on throughout the night, and thus the defenders also worked away. In order to see what was going on, lighted carcasses (tar-filled sacks encased in rope) were used. These brightly burning objects were hurled out from the walls, lighting up the surrounding area for a good many yards and causing all enemy troops in the vicinity to stop work and keep still. These carcasses were, in effect, early forms of the Very Light, which proved so useful in the two world wars. During daylight the defenders would keep up debilitating fire on the besiegers' trenches, both with guns and (when the trenches finally came within range) ordinary musket shot.

The garrison at Burgos is seen here working at repairing the defences and generally manning the walls. Commanded by Dubreton, it proved to be as tenacious as that at Badajoz, the main difference being that the troops at Burgos were successful in repelling Wellington's attacks.

Despite their efforts, the defenders knew that unless a relief force arrived in time they would be forced to face the trial of an assault by enemy troops. Although Dubreton's garrison at Burgos emerged as the only successful French garrison against Wellington's men, the defenders of Badajoz and San Sebastián ran them very close. Phillipon's men denied Wellington in June 1811, whilst Rey's men at San Sebastián withstood the initial assault on the town before it finally fell at the second attempt. At both Badajoz and San Sebastián the defenders put up an extremely tenacious defence, particularly at the former, with all manner of obstacles being placed in the breaches to block them up. Huge logs of wood were placed in each of the breaches at Badajoz, with razor-sharp sword blades sticking out, whilst planks of wood were laid and similarly spiked. Both of these were then chained to the ground to prevent them from being dragged aside. Mines were strategically placed, and crows' feet (vicious iron-spiked objects) were scattered liberally to maim the attackers, whilst at Badajoz the defenders themselves were armed with at least three muskets each, with which they delivered a withering fire on the storm troops when they attacked. The fighting at both San Sebastián and Badajoz was extremely savage, causing the storming troops severe casualties. At Ciudad Rodrigo, however, the resistance was short and feeble, with Wellington's men gaining the two breaches relatively easily after a brief fight by the defenders.

At Burgos, Dubreton's men appear to have been extremely confident of denying the castle to Wellington's men. Throughout the siege in September and October 1812 they demonstrated a dogged determination to upset their enemy's plans, both by sorties and by constant fire which played havoc with the besiegers. When it came to the actual storming, the French demonstrated the sort of determination showed at both Badajoz and San Sebastián, except on this occasion they were successful. It is true that the attacks were delivered by a much smaller force and on a smaller scale, but the defenders were also fewer in number and the defences much weaker. Their prolonged defence allowed French relieving forces to close on Burgos and eventually force Wellington to abandon the siege. Again, buying time was the critical factor. Dubreton achieved it, and through his efforts and those of his defenders they saved themselves from the hulks in England.

In the siege lines

If the sieges in the Peninsula were a trial for the garrisons, they were no less so for the British besiegers who laboured under the great handicaps of not having trained sappers or miners, having insufficient and adequate tools and their operations being frequently hampered by bad weather. Their problems were not made any easier by a lack of experience: Wellington's engineers had never conducted regular siege operations on the scale they were expected to in Spain.

Laying the siege

There were certain requirements essential to any commander before he could contemplate laying siege to a fortress. The first, of course, was an efficient siege train. This meant heavy guns, for without them there was little hope of blasting through walls up to 50ft thick. The most effective siege guns were the huge 24-pounders, with barrels 9ft long, which were capable of hurling a large iron ball over great distances at a rate of one shot per minute, the gunners having to wait a full minute before the smoke from each shot had cleared. These were supported by 18-pounders, although according to Jones, the historian of the sieges in the Peninsula, no self-respecting engineer should settle for 18-pounders when he could obtain 24-pounders, adding that the power of the 24-pounder gun had to be seen to be appreciated. Needless to say, a sufficient supply of ammunition was also needed. In the case of the siege of Badajoz in 1812 there were some 22,367 shells of round shot, and 24,983 shells of various calibres available to the artillery. There were also 2,253 barrels of powder, each weighing 90 lbs.

In order for the trenches to be dug, thousands of tools were also required, including picks and shovels of all shapes and sizes. There also crowbars, cutting tools, vast quantities of nails, wood, tape, saws, sandbags and axes, to name just a few things found amongst the inventory of the engineers' stores at Badajoz.

Of course, the most important requirement for a commander at a siege was manpower. Not only did he require sufficient men to conduct the siege itself, but he also needed enough men to be able to deal with any enemy force that tried to interfere with the siege operations. For example, at the first siege of Badajoz in May

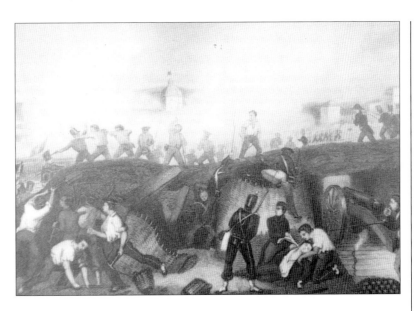

1811, Beresford did not possess enough men for the two and so was forced to abandon the siege when Marshal Soult appeared on the scene, having marched up from Seville to try to relieve the place. No sooner had Beresford marched away from Badajoz to meet Soult, which he did at Albuera on 16 May, than Phillipon marched out of the fortress and filled in all the trenches that Beresford's men had dug to that point. Fortunately for Wellington, he had enough men at the sieges of Ciudad Rodrigo and Badajoz in 1812 and San Sebastián the following year. At Burgos, however, he had barely enough men to conduct the siege operations, let alone fend off the relieving forces.

The business of conducting a siege may have appeared a crude and cumbersome business but, conducted properly, it was a scientific affair. Once identified, the target was reconnoitred, isolated and finally besieged. The process of isolation was essential, it being absolutely essential to stop supplies getting in and messengers getting out. Wellington's engineers, who were commanded by Sir Richard Fletcher, then went about the business of identifying the points considered to be each respective fortress's weak point, in order to determine the siting of the breaching batteries.

Once the besiegers had decided upon the point of attack, the trenches, or parallels as they were called, were traced out with a white line, well out of range of the defenders' guns, and work would begin, usually after dark. This was the process of 'breaking ground', whereby an officer in charge of a working party, the strength of which depended upon the length of ground to be dug, would march in with his men and begin hacking away at the earth, a line of men digging and another piling up the spoil in the form of a rampart for protection. These trenches varied between seven and ten feet in width and were dug by the infantry, who positively hated the work. In their view, when a man joined the British Army he did so in order to fight the French, not dig trenches, which was regarded as navvy's work. It was also a job fraught with danger, as the trenches were constantly under shellfire from the French gunners who all too well knew the range to within a few yards. After all, they could see the trenches quite clearly from their observation posts and it was an easy task for the defenders' artillery to lob shell after shell into the trenches.

Quite often, the weather would be bad, which was the case at all of Wellington's major sieges except for San Sebastián. At Ciudad Rodrigo, snow and fog upset the besiegers, whilst heavy rain did likewise at Badajoz and Burgos. The weather had dire consequences for the besiegers who, instead of being able to pile up the spoil from the trenches to form a kind of rampart, could only watch the

Any aggressive garrison commander worth his salt would see to it that the besiegers' work was delayed as much as possible. The governor of Ciudad Rodrigo, Barrie, proved to be the most inactive of the garrison commanders Wellington encountered. However, he did manage to launch this sortie, on 14 January, the intention being to fill in as much of the besiegers' trenches as possible and carry off their valuable tools.

Burgos Castle and the Hornwork of St Michael, 1812

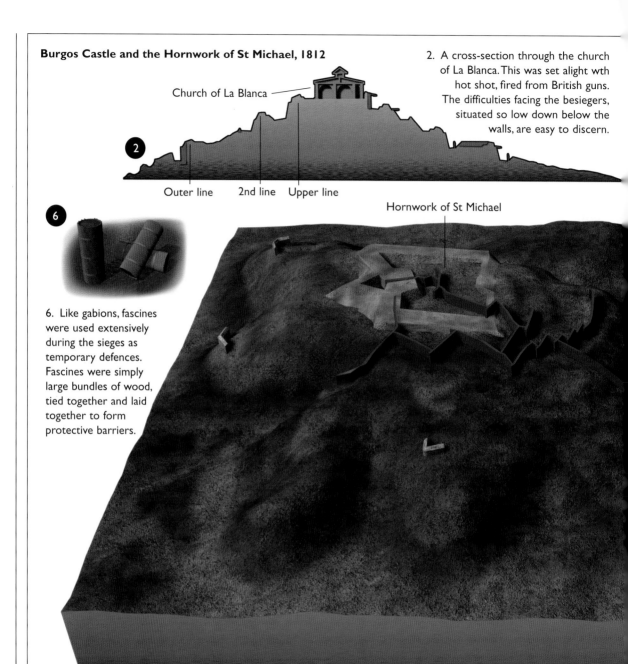

Church of La Blanca

2. A cross-section through the church of La Blanca. This was set alight wth hot shot, fired from British guns. The difficulties facing the besiegers, situated so low down below the walls, are easy to discern.

Outer line   2nd line   Upper line

Hornwork of St Michael

6. Like gabions, fascines were used extensively during the sieges as temporary defences. Fascines were simply large bundles of wood, tied together and laid together to form protective barriers.

Hornwork of St Michael

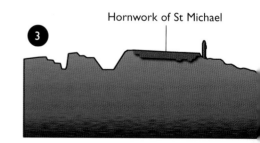

5. Gabions were wickerwork baskets filled with earth and stones. The standard makeshift defensive measure, gabions were usually used to shore up defences which had been damaged by enemy artillery fire.

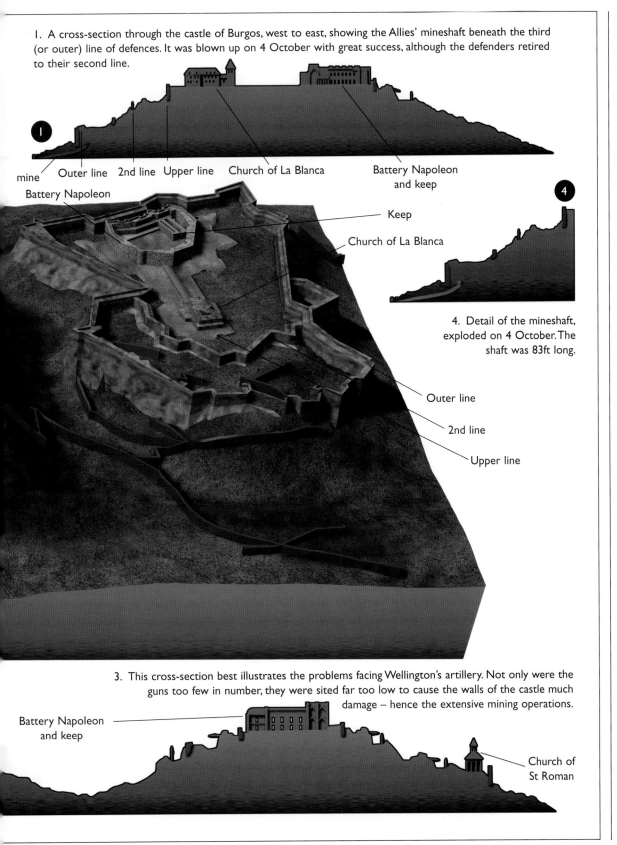

1. A cross-section through the castle of Burgos, west to east, showing the Allies' mineshaft beneath the third (or outer) line of defences. It was blown up on 4 October with great success, although the defenders retired to their second line.

mine   Outer line   2nd line   Upper line   Church of La Blanca   Battery Napoleon and keep

Battery Napoleon

Keep

Church of La Blanca

4. Detail of the mineshaft, exploded on 4 October. The shaft was 83ft long.

Outer line

2nd line

Upper line

3. This cross-section best illustrates the problems facing Wellington's artillery. Not only were the guns too few in number, they were sited far too low to cause the walls of the castle much damage – hence the extensive mining operations.

Battery Napoleon and keep

Church of St Roman

earth turn quickly to liquid mud: this also meant that there was little protection from the enemy's guns. In order to try to suppress the fire coming from them, riflemen were placed in front of the walls in pits, from where their accurate Baker rifles could easily pick off enemy troops who exposed themselves in the embrasures. Commenting on this, John Kincaid, the most famous diarist of the Peninsular War and himself an officer of the 95th Rifles, noted that siege warfare was like a cross between being a gamekeeper and a gravedigger, as it afforded ample employment for both spade and shovel!

Once a trench had been completed the men would begin sapping forward before opening out yet another trench from the sap. By so doing, the besiegers were able to approach the walls of the fortress under the relative cover of these crude earthworks. The next step was to construct the positions from where the guns would fire. The guns needed to be mounted upon wooden platforms, usually 18ft long, with a front some 9ft wide and the rear 18ft wide. The embrasures for the guns were protected by gabions and fascines, although sandbags made excellent substitutes. The security of the trenches was always an important aspect of siege operations, and the greatest vigilance was required: a strong guard had to be present to prevent the enemy from making a sortie against the works. An effective attack by the defenders could seriously retard the siege operations, either by damaging the works or, where tools were in short supply, by carrying off the valuable entrenching tools.

When both the chief engineer and the commander of the artillery were satisfied, the guns were finally given the order to open fire, an occasion usually accompanied by a resounding cheer from the besiegers. It was then down to the skill of the gunners to target and hit the correct section of wall and breach it, in the least possible time, with the minimum expenditure of ammunition, and in the most effective manner. This was of paramount importance, of course, for unless the walls were breached effectively the storming columns would find themselves severely compromised on the night of the assault.

The target for the gunners was the foot of the selected wall and the counterscarp opposite. By hitting the foot of the wall, the masonry would crumble away and, eventually, with the assistance of howitzers that would send high explosives against the target, the wall would collapse into the ditch with the rubble forming a ramp up which the storming columns would attack. If the

Once the engineers had declared the breaches practicable, it fell to the storming columns to carry out the assault. Here, Lt. Maguire of the 4th (King's Own) leads the assault at San Sebastián. He wore a white feather in his cap to make himself conspicuous. Unfortunately, it also made him an easy target and he was killed during the assault.

counterscarp was blown into the ditch too it would make the job of the storming columns immeasurably easier, not that storming was ever viewed as being anything less than a real trial.

Once a breach became severely damaged it was the task of the chief Royal Engineer to decide whether it was practicable or not. This, naturally, was not a decision to make lightly as the lives of hundreds of men depended upon his judgement. Once the decision was taken a plan of attack was drawn up. It was not always a simple case of attacking the breaches. At both Ciudad Rodrigo and Badajoz diversionary attacks were made, the attack on the latter involving an assault by escalade. These attacks were not only designed to draw enemy resources away from the main points of attack, usually the breaches, but were often attacks in their own right against strategic points which Wellington considered practicable.

The test of courage
For all of the scientific nature of approach work during a siege, when it came down to the actual assault it was a simple case of hurling men against the breaches and hoping that, if the engineers and artillery had done their work properly, as few casualties as possible were sustained. Each assault column was preceded by a forlorn hope, often little more than a suicide squad. The size of the forlorn hope could vary anything from 50 to 200 men, led by an officer who, if he was fortunate enough to survive, could look forward to instant promotion. The truth was, however, that he could usually look forward to nothing more than a quick and painful death, for although officers did survive forlorn hopes, such as Gurwood at Ciudad Rodrigo and Dyas (twice) at the San Cristobal at Badajoz, the odds against surviving an assault on a major breach were extremely long indeed.

The poor prospects of survival amongst such men can best be gauged by the forlorn hope's purpose, which was to draw the fire of the defenders and, hopefully (for the main storming columns at least), get them to fire their mines. With any luck, the mines would be exploded early, leaving the main assault columns to deal with the no less dangerous task of gaining the breaches.

Each of the assault columns was preceded by a group of men carrying large sacks filled with grass which were tossed into the ditch in order to break the fall of those coming up behind them. Ladders were also carried. Naturally, it was wise to try to get the men as close as possible to the breaches before being detected, so silence was essential; but with so much equipment being carried forward, and with men stumbling here and there in the darkness, this was not always easy. If the defending garrison was constantly on the alert looking for attacking troops, it was often nigh on impossible. Eventually, both the forlorn hope and the assaulting columns would reach the walls and then it would be quite simply a case of hoping for the best and that, maybe, the defenders would be caught off guard. A successful attack might then just be the end result.

Rights and reputations
We have already examined the decision by French garrisons to fight on, even when practicable breaches had been made in the walls, when, under the old convention of warfare, garrisons would have been expected to surrender. It would not, therefore, be amiss to examine the 'rights' of the attackers after a successful storming, as this has great bearing on the apparent brutal and bad reputation that the British Army gained for itself following the stormings in the Peninsula.

The British troops took a dim view of the decision by the French to carry on fighting, but they fully understood the reasons for it. Furthermore, the British themselves embarked on a similar course of action at Tarifa in 1811–12. Here, at the very tip of Europe, the British defenders fought on even when breaches had been made in the walls. In the event, they were successful in their defence, but it is interesting to consider what might have happened to the garrison if the French had successfully stormed the breaches. Would the French have behaved in the

No matter how thorough the preparations were, it ultimately came down to the ability of the stormers to take a fortress. Here, the men of the 3rd Division lock horns in a ferocious battle with the defenders of the castle at Badajoz. Despite numerous anachronisms regarding uniform, this drawing accurately depicts the savage nature of the hand-to-hand fighting that took place on the ramparts on that memorable night.

same way as British troops at Ciudad Rodrigo, Badajoz and San Sebastián? We will never know. The British troops who stormed these fortresses knew that the breaches were practicable and would have considered it futile for the defenders to carry on. Any casualties sustained during the storming would have been considered by the storming troops to be unnecessary. Thus, they had the right to slaughter the garrison. In the event they did not. Why? Well, one suspects they had other motivations for storming the walls.

We should not forget that Wellington controlled his army by the lash and by the threat of it, and army discipline was rigorous to say the least. When Ciudad Rodrigo was stormed the men found that, suddenly, they were on their own, on the loose in a town in the dead of night, and with no officers able to control them. In the event, the disorder was brief but it gave the men a tremendous taste of what they could expect at Badajoz where, in the much larger town, order would be impossible to maintain. Badajoz suffered from an unfortunate reputation as a place where the population was known to harbour very pro-French feelings, a place where British soldiers had been maltreated in the aftermath of the Battle of Talavera in the summer of 1809. It was also a place that had denied them in 1811, when the attacks on the Fort San Cristobal had been beaten off by the tenacious French garrison. All of these reasons, together with the miseries of the bad weather, conspired to make Badajoz the great prize that it would become for the survivors of the storming. The men needed no drink to scale the walls and attack the breaches, as has often been claimed. No, the motivation lay inside the town where drink was indeed to be found, and in large quantities. Plunder would be easy, murder simple, and debauchery widespread. It was for these reasons, therefore, that not a single man in Wellington's army shrank from the severe test that awaited them on that fateful night in April 1812. John Kincaid of the 95th wrote that, 'such was the rage for passports into eternity, in any battalion, on that occasion, that even the officers' servants insisted on taking their place in the ranks, and I was obliged to leave my baggage in charge of a man who had been wounded some days before.' But perhaps the most chilling description of the assault on Badajoz was written by William Grattan, of the 88th Connaught Rangers, who himself would be wounded in the attack:

The spirits of the soldiers, which no fatigues could dampen, rose to a frightful height. I say frightful because it was not of that sort which alone denoted exultation at the prospect of an exploit which was about to hold them up to the admiration of the world, there was a certain something in their bearing that told plainly they had suffered fatigues, which, though they did not complain of, and had seen their comrades slain while fighting beside them without repining – they smarted under the one, and felt acutely for the other, yet smothered both so long as their bodies and minds were employed; now, however, they had a momentary licence to think, every fine feeling vanished and plunder and revenge took their place … In a word, the capture of Badajoz had long been their idol; many causes led to this wish on their part; the two previous unsuccessful sieges, and the failure of the attack against San Cristobal in the latter; but above all, the well known hostility of its inhabitants to the British army, and perhaps might be added, a desire for plunder which the sacking of Ciudad Rodrigo had given them a taste for. Badajoz was, therefore, denounced as a place to be made example of, and most unquestionably no city, Jerusalem exempted, was ever more strictly visited to the letter than was this ill-fated town.

Badajoz does form a separate case, as there were certainly scores to settle there. But San Sebastián was no less heavily sacked when the place fell in August 1813. Indeed, many British survivors claim that the sacking of San Sebastián was the equal of Badajoz, made worse by the fire that engulfed the town. Whatever the reasons for the behaviour of the British troops after the stormings, to condemn them is to fail to appreciate the enormity of their achievements. Furthermore, it must have been nigh on impossible for the stormers to simply 'switch off' after the attack. Let us not forget that hundreds of British troops were killed and maimed by the fury of the respective assaults, during which men saw their comrades and brothers slaughtered before their very eyes. Should we really condemn them for feeling some degree of bitterness, for wanting to vent their anger upon somebody? The storming of a fortress is not the same as a battle where men expect casualties to occur. But when a force was asked to storm a fortress when practicable breaches had been formed, such casualties would have been deemed unnecessary. Given the enormity of the task facing the stormers in the Peninsula, I for one begrudge them none of their feelings of anger and desire for revenge.

One of the rewards for the successful stormers was the right to sack and plunder the stormed fortress. Here, Wellington is cheered by his men as they enjoy themselves in the streets of Badajoz.

'Sheer bludgeon work': the fortresses in war

In terms of the expenditure of lives, the fighting over these fortresses cost greatly; in terms of the course of the war in the Peninsula, the impact of the fighting was highly significant too. The fortress of Ciudad Rodrigo, commanding as it did the northern corridor between Spain and Portugal and thus of immense importance, was the first of Wellington's successful sieges, and it also proved to be the most straightforward.

Ciudad Rodrigo, as we have noted, was dominated by the Upper Teson, on the forward slope of which was a redoubt. This was taken on the night of 8 January 1812, the first night of the siege. After this, Wellington's men were free to dig trenches and sap forward towards the town's walls, before their guns opened fire to make the breaches. The governor, Barrie, turned in a performance that can at best be described as lacklustre. There was no aggression from him and apart from a single sortie he appears to have relied almost entirely on relieving forces being able to get to him before his command fell. In the event, Barrie was helpless to prevent Wellington's gunners from pounding away at the weak walls and making two practicable breaches, both of which were stormed on the night of 19 January 1812.

On the face of it, there was little that Barrie could have done to save himself once the Upper Teson fell to Wellington. From its lofty position, and from the lower Lesser Teson, the British artillery was able to fire upon the walls of the town without hindrance. With the walls in such a poor state they had little difficulty in breaching both the faussebraie and the walls themselves. Wellington's men suffered none of the disadvantages endured by those at Badajoz, Ciudad's walls being in such a poor condition that it was not necessary for them to dig themselves closer to them; hence, the shortage of entrenching tools was not felt so acutely. Wellington's men were able to dig relatively unhindered and after 11 days the town was won.

The most Barrie could have done was to make more of a resistance on the Upper Teson, and to galvanise his garrison into putting up a better resistance

The storming of the Lesser Breach at Ciudad Rodrigo by the Light Division. The men had little difficulty in mounting the breach and were inside the town in very good time.

on the night of the assault. The walls were indeed weak, but both breaches were not exactly the largest ever seen. The men of the 3rd and Light gained access to the town with relative ease, which would indicate a marked lack of resistance on the part of the garrison. The garrison certainly appear to have been poorly motivated, showing none of the will to fight that one would expect from men facing the likelihood of imprisonment on the dreaded hulks.

Ciudad Rodrigo remained in Allied hands for the rest of the war, giving Wellington command of the northern corridor between the two Iberian nations. He realised all too well the significance of his prize and he would not relinquish it without a fight. In the event, Marmont threatened it only once again, in late April 1812. Thus, Wellington was free to move east–west in the north without fearing for his communications. However, Ciudad Rodrigo was only one of 'the keys to Spain'. The other lay in the south, the mighty fortress town of Badajoz.

On 15 March 1812 Wellington's army appeared in front of the walls of Badajoz to try its luck for a third time. Having been denied twice by Phillipon and his brave garrison in May and June 1811, Wellington's men were hoping it would be third time lucky. Although the fortifications of Badajoz were extremely strong Wellington had never really tested them, for he had not brought the full force of his army to bear upon the fortress. Nor had he undertaken what might be termed a 'fully offensive operation' against the place: the attacks in 1811 were directed against the castle and the Fort San Cristobal. The siege of March and April 1812 would be a very different affair.

Once Badajoz had been isolated and blockaded, Wellington's engineers reconnoitred the place before deciding to direct their main attacks against the bastions of La Trinidad and Santa Maria. In order to do this, and before the breaching batteries could open fire, they would have to dig an extensive system of trenches in front of the walls. Furthermore, they would have to take the strong outwork of Fort Picurina, situated on a slight rise and a perfect site for the breaching batteries to fire on the walls. It was no coincidence that Phillipon had built the fort here: it would deny Wellington use of the space and would cost him valuable time in attacking it, time which would allow two French forces marching to relieve the place to get closer. In the event they would arrive too late to save the garrison, but the construction of the fort was well thought out and its capture cost Wellington many casualties.

Another contemporary version of the storming of Ciudad Rodrigo. Yet again, the men of the Light Division are seen taking the breach, right, by escalade. Interestingly, the key states that the British are attacking the breach in 'Fort Fausse Braie'. This reflects the inaccuracy of these hurried prints that were rushed out soon after news of the event arrived in England. Once again, poor Mackinnon is blown skywards in the background.

Like the defenders of Ciudad Rodrigo and Burgos, the French troops inside Badajoz were ably assisted by the weather, which was extremely bad throughout the first two weeks of the siege. The besiegers had great difficulty in digging their trenches, and there was a notable shortage of entrenching tools too. Indeed, when the French launched their sortie on 19 March Phillipon had offered bounties to any man who brought back such objects. Wellington's chief engineer, Sir Richard Fletcher, was wounded whilst trying to prevent the French from carrying off the tools.

On 25 March Fort Picurina was successfully stormed, thus opening the way for the artillery to install their guns in the main batteries. The huge 24-pounders soon began to take their toll on the walls, which crumbled with every shot. It was during this phase of the siege that Phillipon was at his best, urging his men to make good repairs wherever they could, whilst by night he ordered parties out into the ditches in order to clear away as much of the debris as they could, to deny the besiegers a 'ramp' to climb once the storming finally got underway. Phillipon attended to every detail that would improve his chances of survival and was constantly encouraging his men, urging them on, leading by example. Indeed, he was the epitome of an aggressive commander who was not content with merely sitting back and hoping that when the attack came he would be able to beat it off. Phillipon had defeated Wellington before, and was going to make sure that he did it again. Relieving forces would be on their way, so it was important that the defence was a prolonged one, and he had no reason to think it would be otherwise. Following their heroics the previous year the garrison was well motivated, but Phillipon took care to remind his men of the price of failure, namely the terrible conditions aboard the prison ships, where many could expect to perish through sickness.

Phillipon also made it quite clear that he expected his men to kill as many of the enemy as possible when the assault came. He issued an order to those defending the castle walls along these lines, which stated that 'when the head comes up it comes up unprotected'. Given the attitude of Wellington's men towards the defeated garrison following the successful assault, it is interesting to consider what might have happened to the French had the storming troops been privy to this order.

When the assault on Badajoz finally came, on the memorable and terrible night of 6 April 1812, it was delivered with the full force of Wellington's best divisions; but even they found it impossible to pass through the fiery breaches. It is estimated that over 40 separate attacks were made on the breaches, all without success. Instead, the attackers were simply smashed to pieces in the ditch as they tried desperately to climb up into the breaches. With the walls finally breached Phillipon had resorted to quasi-medieval tactics by blocking up the breaches with *chevaux-de-frise*. Mines were also exploded in the ditches, killing and maiming scores of troops at a stroke. Behind these fearsome defences were lines of French infantrymen who fired into the fiery darkness at very close range, bringing down attacking troops with each volley. It was a nightmarish scene. So successful was the French defence of the breaches that, after the town's eventual capture, it proved almost impossible to pass through the breaches even in daylight and without opposition.

There is no better example of how such fortresses could impact on the outcome of a campaign, certainly in the Peninsula, than Wellington's abortive siege of Burgos in September and October 1812. Having captured both Ciudad Rodrigo and Badajoz by the end of the first week of April 1812, Wellington had command of the two main invasion routes between Spain and Portugal. He was, therefore, perfectly placed to begin his own drive into Spain, which he did in June 1812. The following month he flattened Marmont's French army at Salamanca and on 12 August 1812 he occupied the Spanish capital of Madrid. It was a tremendous and triumphant eight months for him and his army; and yet, the year ended sourly with the infamous retreat to Portugal in October and November, with Wellington exactly where he had started, back on the Portuguese border. This reversal was purely the result of his failure to capture the castle of Burgos.

A contemporary version of the storming of Badajoz. Picton's 3rd Division escalades the walls of the castle (right), while the 4th and Light divisions attack the three breaches (centre left). A night of fire and blood is well depicted in this effective scene.

When Wellington marched on Madrid, he did so largely for political rather than military reasons. After defeating Marmont at Salamanca the logical route was to the north-east, where the long road to France beckoned him onwards. Only Valladolid, Burgos and Vittoria lay between him and the sacred soil of France, and with the opposition scattered following his great victory of 22 July 1812 this appeared to be the logical route. Yet Wellington, ever the soldier-diplomat, chose to liberate Madrid. There were sound reasons for this, but in the event it proved to be a flawed decision.

With Madrid secure Wellington finally cast his eyes to the north-east, to Burgos and the great road to France. Reports indicated that Burgos would not trouble him unduly. After all, it was not like Badajoz or Ciudad Rodrigo, whose walls had cost him time, energy and manpower. On the contrary, Burgos was an open town with the French garrison ensconced within the unsophisticated walls of the old castle. Surely he would not need the services of his storming divisions, the 3rd, 4th and Light? He marched north with the intention of employing the 1st and 6th divisions and two Portuguese brigades as his besieging troops with the veterans of the 5th Division, supported by the 7th Division acting as a covering force to the north-east of Burgos. Given the size of the target it could be argued that this constituted an adequate force; but it was the lack of guns which really cost him dear. Wellington marched north with just three 18-pounders and five 24-pounders, the latter proving to be wholly inadequate.

A later, but nevertheless accurate, depiction of the Light Division at Badajoz. The men are seen here dropping into the ditch, a task in itself, before moving against the breaches.

The first objective for Wellington was the capture of the hornwork on the heights of St Michael, which overlooked the castle. This was accomplished on the night of 19 September but not without the loss of over 400 officers and men. With sufficient heavy guns at his disposal Wellington would have been able to pound away at the walls from the newly secured hornwork; but with just a handful of guns it proved an impossible task. Instead, the siege of Burgos was marked by a great deal of mining operations as Wellington's men strove to blow up the walls from close quarters, rather than undertake the usual method of digging trenches, sapping and constructing breaching batteries.

In the event neither mining nor guns proved effective, and with little progress being made Wellington was forced to resort to throwing men against the walls and into the woefully small breaches in the hope that through sheer guts and determination they might make good the deficiencies of the other arms. It was a vain hope. The garrison, some 2,000-strong, proved worthy opponents and had little difficulty in throwing back the despairing Allied attacks. Throughout the siege the French conducted their own counter-mining operations and launched several effective sorties, destroying large sections of the Allied works. There were major assaults by Wellington's men on 22 September and again on 4 and 18 October, but they were repulsed by the French with loss. The last great assault on 18 October was vividly described by John Mills, an officer with the Coldstream Guards, in his diary, the day after the attack:

At three o'clock it was communicated to us that the place was to be stormed at 4 o'clock. The signal was the explosion of the mine, on which a flag was to be held up on the hill. The mine exploded – the explosion was attended with so little noise that though we were anxiously expecting it, we could hear no noise. The earth shook a little, we looked to the hill and saw the flag. The 300 Germans stormed the breach and got well up it. They then attempted the third line, by a place in the wall which was broken down. It ended with their being beat out of the whole with the loss of 7 officers and a great many men. Our party was to escalade the wall in front. Burgess ran forward with 30 men, Walpole and myself followed with fifty each and ladders. Burgess got up without much difficulty, Walpole and myself followed. The place we stood on was a ledge in the wall about three feet from the top. A most tremendous fire opened upon us from every part which took us in front and rear. They poured down fresh men and ours kept falling down into the ditch, dragging and knocking down others. We were so close that they fairly put their muskets into our faces, and we pulled one of their men through an embrasure. Burgess was killed and Walpole severely wounded. We had hardly any men left on the top and at last we gave way. How we got over the palisades I know not. They increased their fire as we retreated, and we came off with the loss of more than half our party and all the badly wounded were left in the ditch. Burgess behaved nobly – he was the first up the ladder and waved his hat on the top. I found him lying there wounded. He begged me to get my men up and in the act of speaking a stone hit him, he fell on the ledge and was shot dead. The time we were on the wall was not more than six minutes. The fire was tremendous, shot, shells, grape, musketry, large stones, hand grenades and every missile weapon was used against us.

The failure of these attacks proved fatal to Wellington's assault, and there is no reason to suspect that subsequent attacks would have fared any better, even with reinforcements in terms of guns and manpower. However, given time it is likely that the commander Dubreton and his garrison would have been forced to surrender through starvation, isolated as they were high above the town. We should not forget the time factor here though: the time bought by the garrison

Badajoz may well have been taken by storm, as the caption of this contemporary print indicates, but the successful attacks did not occur at the breaches. Here, British troops are seen storming a breach, whilst French troops defend it successfully.

San Sebastián, 1813

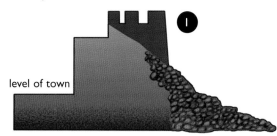

level of town

Distribution of Allied artillery, 26 August 1813: the left attack		
Battery	**Pieces**	**Target**
No.5	6 x 18pdrs	To breach the east demi-bastion of the high curtain
No.6	7 x 24pdrs	To breach the east demi-bastion of the high curtain
	2 x 8in. howitzers	To breach the east demi-bastion of the high curtain

1. A section through the breach in the tower at the right-hand end of the curtain wall (see main illustration for location).

Following the storming on 31 August, a new battery was established in the captured hornwork, to fire upon the castle.

The castle

6. The small island of Santa Clara was taken on 26 August by the naval squadron and 200 men of the 9th Foot. Battery No.10 was established on this island.

5. Allied artillery batteries 3–7. The guns here opened the breach in front of the hornwork. Battery No.7 also fired upon the breaches in the eastern wall.

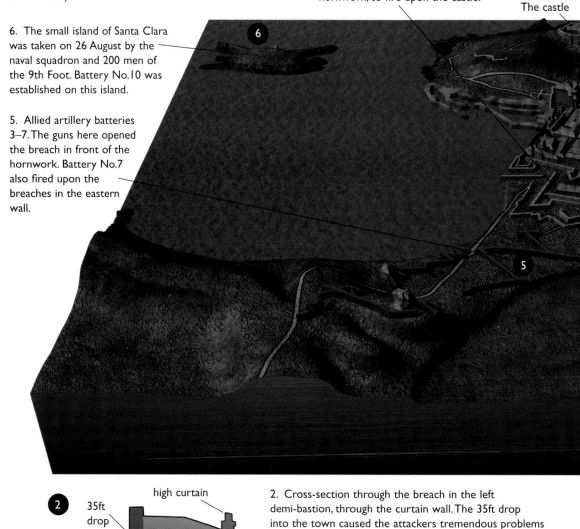

2. Cross-section through the breach in the left demi-bastion, through the curtain wall. The 35ft drop into the town caused the attackers tremendous problems on 31 August.

35ft drop

high curtain

level of town

breach in demi-bastion

The right attack		
Battery	Pieces	Target
No.11	2 x 8in. howitzers	general fire on defences
No.13	1 x 12in. mortar	rear of breach, town and castle
	5 x 10in. mortars	rear of breach, town and castle
No.14	6 x 24pdrs	the breaches
	5 x 8in. howitzers	enfilade fire on curtain wall and land front
	4 x 68pdr carronades	enfilade fire on curtain wall and land front

The right attack (cont.)		
Battery	Pieces	Target
No.15	15 x 24pdrs	the breaches
No.16	4 x 10in. mortars	the land front and castle

Monte Urgullo

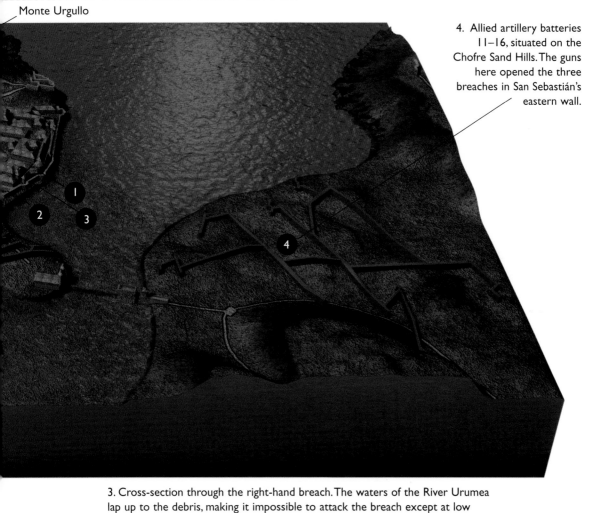

4. Allied artillery batteries 11–16, situated on the Chofre Sand Hills. The guns here opened the three breaches in San Sebastián's eastern wall.

3. Cross-section through the right-hand breach. The waters of the River Urumea lap up to the debris, making it impossible to attack the breach except at low tide. The breach is retrenched, thus giving the attackers yet another barrier to pass, even after they have carried the first breach.

debris

Wellington's men went well and truly beyond the call of duty at the escalade of both the San Vicente bastion and the castle walls at Badajoz. Here, Leith's 5th Division scales the walls of the San Vicente bastion, despite having ladders that were far too short. The men stand on each other's shoulders to reach the top, in the face of fierce resistance from the French who, in the event, were powerless to stop the British troops from gaining the ramparts. A truly remarkable feat of bravery.

allowed French relieving troops to close on the town and force Wellington to abandon the siege altogether. Thus on 21 October the Allies began to withdraw from the place.

The attack on Burgos proved to be Wellington's one great defeat in the Peninsula, largely the result of a combination of a lack of engineers, guns and experienced troops, although nobody could have given more than the Foot Guards, the 24th Foot and the King's German Legion. The defeat was also a result of the French having an extremely determined garrison in Burgos, commanded by an equally aggressive commander. The bad weather did not help Wellington either, with the infantry, who hated siege work, growing ever more exasperated by the dreadful conditions in the trenches.

The siege of Burgos perfectly bears out Napoleon's maxim that 'fortresses alone will not win a war but a successful defence will retard the movements of an enemy'. In fact, one might argue that the tenacious defence of Burgos by Dubreton almost did win the war for the French, as many of Wellington's officers, demoralised and shocked by the episode, considered it to be as good as over. With little prospect of victory, they said, there was no point in remaining in Spain any longer. John Mills's comments are worthy of note:

Our want of success at Burgos and the subsequent retreat will cause a great deal of dissatisfaction in England. I think it has turned the tide of affairs here and Spain I think is lost. If ever a man ruined himself the Marquis [Wellington] has done it; for the last two months he has acted like a madman. The reputation he has acquired will not bear him out – such is the opinion here.

Fortunately for Wellington, his army demonstrated its great power of recovery and by spring the following year was sufficiently recovered to advance into Spain yet again and bring about an eventual Allied victory. However, on this occasion Wellington made certain that, rather than attack Burgos, he outflanked it and forced the French to blow up the castle and retreat. It was not a course of action he had considered in 1812 but the Vittoria campaign of 1813 was marked by a long march to the north of the great road, avoiding it and outflanking successive French positions that barred his way.

In the summer of 1813, following the victory at Vittoria, Wellington's army continued north along the great road to France, drawing up along a front which extended from the coast (marking Wellington's left flank) to Roncesvalles in the Pyrenees (marking his right). The main road into France through the Western Pyrenees was protected by the fortress of San Sebastián, to which Wellington laid siege in July and August 1813. Wellington could not contemplate an invasion of France without taking the town, threatening as it did his communications with Spain. Also, with Marshal Suchet still fighting in the east of the country, there was always the possibility that he might fall upon Wellington's right rear. Thus, the decision was taken to lay siege to the place.

The siege of San Sebastián certainly cost Wellington time, not to mention heavy casualties, but the operation did not retard Wellington's campaign in the north significantly, save for a delay in the eventual invasion of France. Again, the events exposed the British Army's lack of trained engineers and of a corps of sappers and miners. The army was once more forced to rely on the brawn of the ordinary line infantry to labour in the trenches before the town, supervised by their own officers who in turn were supervised by a woefully small number of Royal Engineers officers. This small but brave band of professional soldiers was once again hard pushed to conduct operations with limited manpower and tools at their disposal. Furthermore, they were forced to place themselves in the line of fire in order to ensure that everything went according to plan in the trenches. This resulted in the death of Wellington's chief engineer, Sir Richard Fletcher, who was killed in the trenches by an enemy musket ball.

The governor of San Sebastián, General Rey, may have lacked the aggressive spirit of Phillipon but he certainly had more bite than Barrie had demonstrated at Ciudad Rodrigo. He defied the British storming columns on 25 July, and in fact held his enemies at bay long enough for Marshal Soult, commanding the French just across the border, to launch an attack that he hoped would relieve San Sebastián. In the event, this attack took place on the very day that the town fell, notwithstanding the fact that Soult's operation failed anyway.

Sir Thomas Graham oversaw the siege operations at San Sebastián, as Wellington was forced to keep one eye on the Pyrenees, where the French attacked in late-July 1813. Graham, a more than able deputy, did his best in what was a difficult operation. The geographical setting of San Sebastián, jutting as it did into the Bay of Biscay,

The storming of San Sebastián, 31 August 1813. The assault here appears to be taking place at night, whereas it actually took place in broad daylight. The men had to wade across the wide River Urumea to attack the breaches. Like Badajoz, the town was thoroughly sacked afterwards.

meant that it could never be totally cut off and blockaded: a band of brave and very elusive French seamen managed to evade British ships and supply the garrison by sea.

Despite the great difficulties of trying to besiege a town covered by water on three sides, the siege pressed on. On 31 August 1813, Graham was ready to launch another assault. The failed assault of the previous month had resulted in veiled criticisms of the 5th Division, which had attempted the attack. Sir James Leith, the divisional commander, had been home on leave during the first assault and returned to find his men still peeved at the negative comments. Indeed, there was a suggestion that another division would be called up to make the second attack, but Leith would have none of it. There was too much at stake for this proud Scotsman and he saw to it that his division had the honour of attacking San Sebastián a second time.

The assault on 31 August was unique in the annals of the Peninsular War as it took place in broad daylight. There was no real attempt made to surprise the garrison, not that surprise could ever have been achieved given that the Portuguese storming columns had to wade across almost 500 yards of water at the mouth of the River Urumea to attack the walls. In the event, the assault was successful, but the storming columns met with stiff opposition from the defenders. Indeed, the British and Portuguese troops were flung back to the foot of the breached sea wall and the attack stalled. From his position in the Allied lines, Graham could clearly see what was happening and what needed to be done. In an unusual move, he ordered his artillery to fire over the heads of the assaulting troops at the defenders on the ramparts. One can almost imagine the shock and surprise of the stormers as shell after shell came crashing in low over their heads. It could almost be seen as an early form of the creeping barrage, and it worked. As the stormers pressed their heads into the ground the shells rained in above them, decapitating most of the defenders exposed on the ramparts. Indeed, it was noted afterwards by the British troops just how many of the defenders lay dead and headless.

With the defenders forced back by Allied artillery fire, the storming troops were able to gain the top of the breach. Even here, though, despite the absence of any armed resistance, they had difficulty in gaining entrance to the town on account of a deep retrenchment that Rey had ordered to be made behind the breach. The first British officers to mount the breach found it isolated from the interior of the town by a drop of about 30ft, and the first man to jump down broke his back doing so. In the event, the drop caused only a temporary delay to the stormers who soon broke into the town, driving the defenders to a fort situated atop Monte Urgullo. Here they held out for another week, before surrendering on 7 September. In the meantime, the successful stormers embarked upon yet another ritual sacking.

Another view of the storming of San Sebastián. Once the town had fallen to Wellington's men, Rey and the survivors of his garrison retreated to the castle at the top of Monte Urgullo, where they surrendered a week later.

The fortresses today

Today's visitor to the fortresses of the Peninsular War will find them largely intact and worth extensive exploration. The real gem is Ciudad Rodrigo, which has undergone no real changes since the heady days of 1812. Burgos too has not suffered the sort of development that has resulted in massive changes to both San Sebastián and Badajoz. All four retain elements of the kind of fortifications that we have examined in this book, in varying states of preservation.

Ciudad Rodrigo is the most satisfying fortress to visit as it retains all of its walls. Indeed, it is still possible to walk a complete circuit of the ramparts. One of the first things when visiting any fortress, or for that matter, any battlefield, is to orientate oneself. At Ciudad Rodrigo this means a climb to the top of the Upper Teson in order to obtain the sort of view which Wellington's gunners had. It is also a necessary climb if one wishes to see the remaining earthworks thrown up by Wellington on the plateau of the Teson. The visitor will see how the forts, with their deep ditches, would have linked together to delay any attacking force that wished to use the Teson to site its guns. And when one stands on the forward slope of the Upper Teson one can appreciate immediately just how much of a weakpoint the Upper and Lower Tesons really were. Sadly, the Lower Teson, from where Wellington's artillery did most damage of all, is today covered almost entirely by several ugly blocks of apartments which make it impossible to get the same view that Wellington's forward batteries had. At this point, one can only envy the American historian, Jac Weller, who was able to visit and photograph

The site of the Great Breach in the Trinidad bastion, Badajoz. Until a few years ago the year 1812 was picked out with cannon balls high on the wall. They have since disappeared but it is still possible to see the holes. Many brave men are interred inside the breach.

Fort San Cristobal, Badajoz, as seen from the covered way. The glacis rolls away behind the camera, effectively shielding all that is visible in this photo. It is a most effective glacis.

Ciudad Rodrigo before the buildings were constructed. Indeed, one of his photos is featured in his excellent book, *Wellington in the Peninsula*.

But it is not all doom and gloom on the Lower Teson. From its right-hand end it is still possible to get the view that some of Wellington's batteries had back in January 1812, and to appreciate the accuracy of the British artillery fire, which created two breaches in the walls. The Great Breach does not seem particularly difficult to hit, but the Lesser Breach certainly does. Indeed, to have hit the foot of the walls from such a range is a great testament to the prowess of the artillery; although when one sees the damage to the cathedral, situated directly behind the breaches, and to the walls of the neighbouring buildings, the admiration may be somewhat tempered!

From the Tesons the visitor should now walk through the site of the Lesser Breach, which today is one of the main entrances into the town. In 1812, a tower stood here, and it was the demolition of this tower, and of the adjoining walls, that provided the Light Division with its target on the night of 19 January 1812. Today, it is still possible to work out the original line of the walls by following the course of the faussebraie, which juts forward away from the wall in front of the breach. Naturally, in 1812, the wall and tower jutted forward too, but not any more. It is possible to stand in the many embrasures on the ramparts in order to get a defender's view of the British attack. It is also possible to walk outside the walls and explore the ditch and the faussebraie. This immense bank of earth looks remarkably formidable today, but its undoing was the accuracy of Wellington's artillery, which caused a great deal of damage to it, rendering it relatively easy to pass on the night of the storming.

By walking along the ramparts from the Lesser Breach the visitor reaches the site of the Great Breach, the size of which can still easily be judged by the repair work carried out after the siege. There are, of course, no traces whatsoever of the ditches that the French cut in order to isolate the breach from the interior of the town, although it is not difficult to understand how this worked. Looking out over the glacis and the ditches, one has to admire the great efforts made by the storming troops and wonder why the French defenders did not put up more of a fight.

Continuing along the ramparts towards the River Agueda will bring the visitor to the castle, now a *parador*, one of the excellent state-run hotels. It was here that Governor Barrie surrendered his sword to John Gurwood of the 52nd, although Lt. Mackie of the 88th has an equally strong claim to have been the first man inside the castle. Today, a pleasant garden occupies the position where the two guns, which would have enfiladed the attacking 5th and 94th regiments, were sited. It is at this point that one begins to appreciate how Wellington's overall plan fell out, and just how important it was for O'Toole and his men to silence these two guns.

If visiting Ciudad Rodrigo, the visitor should make the extra journey across the Portuguese border to see the beautifully preserved town of Almeida. A superb fortress town, albeit a small one, Almeida was the twin of Ciudad Rodrigo and protected the northern corridor between Spain and Portugal on the latter's side of the border. Almeida is the true embodiment of a Vauban fortress, with wonderful angles, bastions, ravelins, a wide ditch and all manner of defensive innovations. The sad thing about Almeida is that we will never know how it would have stood up to a major siege, as it fell to the French in the most unfortunate manner. Wellington, whose army had already started to retreat towards Lisbon, had hoped that the defence of the fortress by a Portuguese garrison commanded by a British officer would buy him enough time to put distance between his own army and Masséna's. Wellington needed this time for his engineers to complete the Lines of Torres Vedras. Marshal Ney duly arrived before Almeida in August 1810 and after digging an extensive set of trenches before the town, opened fire on the 24th of the same month. As luck would have it, one of the first shots fired by the French guns ignited the powder magazine, which exploded massively, killing over 500 men. The fortifications were still relatively steady but the garrison was, naturally, shaken and sued for terms the next day. Thus the fortress fell without any trouble at all to the French and without the need for a prolonged siege and assault. A visit to Almeida is a must for any visitor to the battlefields of the Peninsular War and of fortifications in particular.

The three other fortresses featured in this book have suffered appreciably over the years. The mighty walls of Badajoz still look as strong as ever, although large sections have long since been pulled down. Fortunately, the area of the breaches remains largely intact, although a road has been driven through the curtain wall between the Trinidad and Santa Maria bastions. The castle is as lofty as ever, and standing on the walls one is moved to ask how the French ever allowed the Allied stormers to scale the walls. The same goes for the San Vicente bastion. This remains in good condition although the walls are appreciably lower here than at the castle. The ditches, the elaborate network of ravelins, and the glacis have long since been removed; thus we are unable to gauge the true strength of the fortress. It remains a forbidding place nevertheless.

Burgos was largely destroyed by the French when they abandoned the place during Wellington's advance to Vittoria in June 1813. It is, therefore, difficult to appreciate its real strength. However, the three lines of defences outside its immediate walls can be defined with ease. In fact, a car park lies between two of the lines. The hornwork stands high on the hill over-looking the remains of the castle, although trees obscure the view across the gorge between the two. Nevertheless, with Jones' maps at hand, Burgos is well worth a visit and visitors will certainly be rewarded if they apply themselves to the task of identifying the fortifications.

San Sebastián was largely destroyed by the fire that followed the storming of the town on 31 August 1813, and has suffered similarly over the years with the expansion of the town. Today, San Sebastián is a rather smart Spanish resort and all traces of the defences that defied Wellington and Graham have long since gone. The Urumea has been canalised, making it impossible to cross the river, whilst only the sea wall gives a hint of past defences. Memorials can be found on Monte Urgullo, although some of these are to British soldiers who fought in the Carlist Wars.

The outer ditch and faussebraie at Ciudad Rodrigo. In the left background is the site of the Lesser Breach, stormed by the Light Division. Robert 'Black Bob' Craufurd lies buried beneath it.

Further reading

Surprisingly – or perhaps not, given the relatively unsatisfactory nature of Wellington's sieges – little has been written about siege warfare in the Peninsula. The natural place to begin any study is with Maj. Gen. Sir John T. Jones's *Journal of the Sieges Carried on by the Army under The Duke of Wellington in Spain, during the years 1811 to 1814*. It was first published in 1814 in a single volume, but in 1846 a three-volume edition appeared, massively enlarged and with the addition of a whole volume focussing on the Lines of Torres Vedras. Jones had been a Royal Engineers officer in the Peninsula and his observations are extremely important. Not only do they cover the basic principles of siege warfare and fortification in general, but they also address issues relating to artillery and the need for correct and effective guns, without which it would have been impossible to breach the walls of the fortresses.

The *Dickson Manuscripts*, being the *Diaries, Letters, Maps, Account Books*, with various other papers, published in Woolwich in 1905, are another very important source of information relating to the sieges. Edited by Maj. John Leslie, they comprise the papers of Maj. Gen. Alexander Dickson of the Royal Artillery. The chapters covering the arrangements made by the Royal Artillery for the sieges are very useful indeed. There are few diaries written by engineers who served in the Peninsula, although the two-volume work *The Life and Correspondence of Field Marshal Sir John Burgoyne, Bart.*, edited by his son-in-law Lt. Col. the Hon. George Wrottesley and published in 1873, is of great use.

Specific works on individual siege operations themselves are even more rare. My own *In Hell before Daylight*, first published in 1984, covers the third siege of Badajoz, as does my Osprey Campaign Series title, *Badajoz 1812*, which also deals with Ciudad Rodrigo. Sir Charles Oman's *Wellington's Army*, published in London in 1913, also has a useful section on Wellington's sieges. Don Horward's oddly titled *Napoleon and Iberia: The Twin Sieges of Ciudad Rodrigo and Almeida*, published in Tallahassee in 1984, has little to do with Wellington's siege operations but is a good account of how the French conducted their operations.

Naturally, detailed accounts of the sieges can be found in the three classic accounts of the war: William Napier's six-volume *History of the War in the Peninsula*, published from 1828 onwards; Sir Charles Oman's seven-volume *History of the Peninsular War*, published from 1902 onwards; and in Volumes 6–10 of Sir John Fortescue's *History of the British Army*, published between 1910 and 1920. Jac Weller's *Wellington in the Peninsula*, published in 1962, is probably the best single-volume history of the war and contains good accounts of the sieges. Two other very important works are, of course, *Wellington's Despatches* and *Supplementary Despatches*, which were published in London in 1832 and 1857 respectively. In these multi-volume works are to be found the majority of Wellington's own correspondence relating to all matters, including the sieges.

Glossary

A simplified list of definitions is provided below. An expanded treatment of key terms, based on the *Instructions for Officers and Infantry, showing How to Trace and Construct all sorts of Field Works* by Gen. F. Gaudi (translated into English by C. Marorti de Martemont and published in 1804), can be found in Fortress 7, *The Lines of Torres Vedras 1809–11*.

Banquette A raised step on the inside of a rampart, from which the defenders can fire on the enemy.

Bastion A stronghold, that when linked together with other bastions forms an enclosure around a city or town.

Breach An opening made in the wall or rampart of a fortified place.

Chevaux-de-frise Large pieces of wood full of spikes, sword blades or long nails. These were used to block up breaches and to prevent access to enemy troops.

Cordon A course of stones where the parapet meets the rampart.

Counterscarp The sloping edge of a ditch nearest to the besiegers.

Cunette A trench along the middle of a ditch, serving as an obstacle or a drain.

Curtain A wall that joins together two bastions.

Ditch A hollow channel made beyond the rampart, which extends all the way around the fortifcation. The edges of the ditch are made to slope, with the slope nearest the fortification called the *scarp* and the slope nearest the besiegers called the *counterscarp*.

Embrasure An opening made in a fortification through which guns or muskets are fired.

Fascine An object made of bundles of branches like faggots, some 6ft long and tied in two places. Used to strengthen or replace walls of trenches or other places.

Faussebraie An artificial mound or wall erected in front of the main rampart.

Gabion A kind of basket c.3ft high and usually of the same diameter, filled with earth and used to provide cover during sieges.

Glacis The sloping ground immediately before the ditch, over which attacking forces would pass before descending into it.

Hornwork An outwork consisting of two demi-bastions connected by a curtain wall and joined to the main work by two parallel wings.

Lunette A work placed on both sides of a ravelin to defend it; or, simply, a small fort.

Palisades Strong wooden stakes c.9ft long, driven into the ground, and usually covered, and situated about a yard from the parapet of the glacis.

Parallel A deep trench in which the troops working on the approaches to a fortified place can be supported.

Parapet A bank of earth raised upon the outer edge of a rampart. Used to protect the besieged and to give cover to the defenders to enable them to fire down into the ditch.

Rampart A masonry wall or a great bank of earth around a town or city.

Ravelin A work placed in front of a curtain wall and used to cover the flanks of a bastion.

Retrenchment A fortification consisting of a trench and a parapet; usually, an inner line of defence within a large work.

Saps Trenches made under cover of gabions, fascines, etc. and pushed forward from the main parallel to establish batteries and other parallels.

Scarp The sloping edge of a ditch nearest to the fortification.

Talus The sloping side of a wall or earthwork.

Terreplein A sloping bank of earth behind a parapet.

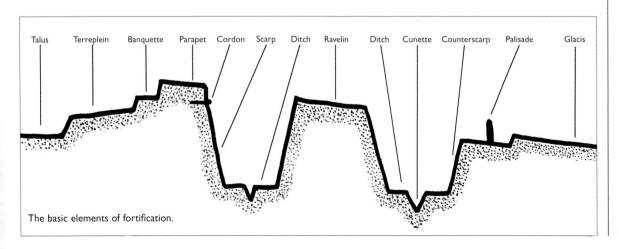

The basic elements of fortification.

Index

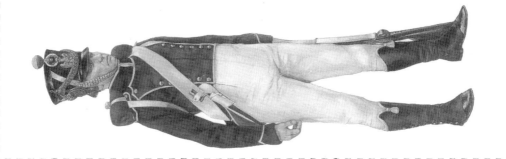

FIND OUT MORE ABOUT OSPREY

❏ Please send me the latest listing of Osprey's publications

❏ I would like to subscribe to Osprey's e-mail newsletter

Title / rank _____

Name _____

Address _____

_____

City / county _____

Postcode / zip _____ state / country _____

e-mail _____

I am interested in:

❏ Ancient world
❏ Medieval world
❏ 16th century
❏ 17th century
❏ 18th century
❏ Napoleonic
❏ 19th century

❏ American Civil War
❏ World War 1
❏ World War 2
❏ Modern warfare
❏ Military aviation
❏ Naval warfare

Please send to:

USA & Canada:
Osprey Direct USA, c/o MBI Publishing, P.O. Box 1, 729 Prospect Avenue, Osceola, WI 54020

UK, Europe and rest of world:
Osprey Direct UK, P.O. Box 140, Wellingborough, Northants, NN8 2FA, United Kingdom

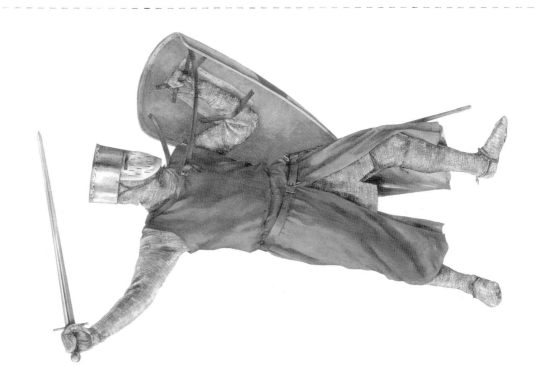

www.ospreypublishing.com

call our telephone hotline
for a free information pack

USA & Canada: 1-800-826-6600
UK, Europe and rest of world call:
+44 (0) 1933 443 863

Young Guardsman
Figure taken from Warrior 22:
Imperial Guardsman 1799–1815
Published by Osprey
Illustrated by Christa Hook

Knight, c.1190
Figure taken from *Warrior 1: Norman Knight 950 – 1204 AD*
Published by Osprey
Illustrated by Christa Hook

POSTCARD

www.ospreypublishing.com